EXPECTING HEAVEN...

Please check out my website and leave
your comments, reviews and ratings at
www.expectingheaven.com
or my Facebook page

Helen Brown

Expecting Heaven...
Copyright © 2022 by Helen Brown

Tellwell Talent
www.tellwell.ca

ISBN
978-0-2288-7370-9 (Hardcover)
978-0-2288-7369-3 (Paperback)
978-0-2288-7699-1 (eBook)

Table of Contents

Introduction

Like many of you, I've spent most of my existence struggling with life, God, and doubt. We seem to be on a never-ending quest for true happiness, questioning our identity and purpose, desperately searching for an inner source of joy because the world never seems to provide us with enough.

Why is this? We choose many different paths, trying them out for a time, hoping that we have found the 'one' that will finally bring us peace, only to be once again disappointed by that path after the initiation.

During this process, I discovered that the majority's consensus does not define truth. So much of what we do today to maintain some sense of joy is merely cosmetic. It keeps us happy for a time, but then fades away because it's not deeply rooted in anything.

However, truth is found in understanding. Understanding of how we got here, who we really are, and why? This true awakening of discernment unveils the most inexplicable sensation of peace that has been gifted to each one of us; and it is God's promise that this joy is only a taste of what is to come in Heaven.

In the pages ahead, we are going to explore the truth about life and look at the obvious and overwhelming evidence of God's design, not only through science and literature, but through God's own words found in the Bible.

This world is not an accident that has produced us from nothing. We have been entrusted with this earth and this life, but more importantly, we have also been assigned the responsibility of giving credit to the creator of it. **God.**

"For with God nothing shall be impossible."
Luke 1:37

Preface

Life tends to be continually busy until someone we love passes away. Then our world stops. During our sadness for a diminished amount of time, we question, "Where did they go?" And then, almost instantly, we step right back into our hurried lives.

When I lost my mom, the person who had always been in my life, it genuinely affected me. All that remains is her grave site and memories. Where did that beautiful soul go, the essence of who she was?

Everyone has a different answer to this question, but only ONE can be correct. The search for the truth never seems simple, yet the path to heaven is. All you have to realize is the importance of finding that path.

Whether or not you believe in God, humble yourself, close your eyes and have a chat with him for a few moments. Ask God to reveal himself to you. Be sincere. God has been patiently waiting for you.

His door is always open; we just have to walk in.

Chapter One
Questions

Sir, my concern is not whether God is on our side: my concern, is to be on God's side, for God is always right.
— Abraham Lincoln

We all have questions about our lives and the world we live in. Big questions, such as: Is God for real? What about evolution and creation? What happens when we die? Are Heaven and Hell real? How can we be certain of an afterlife? What do you suppose is holding us back from having complete confidence in the answers? We always feel as if we can never know them for certain.

Some of the greatest analytical minds in history have also wrestled with these questions, and there are many complicated views, but most of these big questions have surprisingly simple answers, and it is the validation for these answers that I wish to demonstrate to you.

So, let's begin with the basics... hopefully explained in a way you have never heard before.

Most people in the world have never heard 'real' Christianity, although we hear religious talk all the time. Religion is almost always hypocritically spoken, and that hypocrisy, unquestionably, turns us away from God... for very good reason.

However, I believe the majority of us are at least curious about God; the world has always talked about God and countless people believe he is real, so why wouldn't we be curious about him?

Historically, God was a very important part of everyday life. Most of our forefathers believed in God and prayed frequently throughout the day, whether for family members, a good crop, or simply surviving a cold and harsh winter; almost everyone in those days had an unquestioning faith in God. It didn't really matter what they prayed for, they just prayed and believed.

So, what has changed?

In today's culture, generally speaking, life is good and times are good. We have jobs, food, and enough money to buy whatever we want. So, why would we need God?

Humans believe they have complete control over their careers, family, and vacations, choosing the right place to live, in the ideal house, with the perfect dog.

We don't require the presence of God. We've got this...

At the same time, church attendance is dwindling, and parents no longer see the need to teach their children about the Bible. They would rather let children 'select' their own beliefs as they get older, because the modern world is all about individual choice.

In the meantime, prayer has been banned in schools. Not only banned, but downright outlawed, and any talk of God or religion is no longer tolerated. Which is ironic given that society waves the 'tolerance' flag in our face.

The other more serious aspect of this conversion, however, is the strengthening of the atheist belief system as a result of evolution education. Educators give support to atheism instead of creation by prohibiting God from being taught in schools and then use the word 'fact' in reference to evolutionary science, but that couldn't be further from reality.

This so-called 'applied science' is based solely on subjective observational science, and is, for the most part, an educated guess from the scientists and archaeologists that propagate this notion as reality.

These theories and explanations, which are taught in schools and written in textbooks, tend to get increasingly more crazy and complicated in order to fit the narrative. Students wholeheartedly believe what they are being told and sadly there is no option in public education for questioning what is being taught.

However, the real purpose of teaching this

narrative is to align the education system with "D*arwin's Theory of Evolution."* The theories written by Charles Darwin have been written as if they were fact-based. Not true. In the following chapters, I'll go through this in detail.

One of the biggest problems with the modern age we live in is that we have lost the ability to hold a discussion on education... on anything actually.

Enter the modern day 'cancel culture'. People literally hold their hands up and say, "I don't want to talk about it." They cancel discussion, conversation, debate, and today, they even cancel history like it never happened.

For example, for fear of offending someone, this culture removes anything that represents the past and how we have historically arrived at this point. We are no longer able to learn from or discuss those historical times. Similarly, teaching about past wars and conquered societies in education is becoming obsolete.

This isn't right. You cannot wipe the historical slate clean because the things that happened at that time would not be acceptable today. These events happened, and at the time they did so with valid reasons. Countless people fought and lost their lives for our freedom. At the very least, we should be able to respectfully talk about our past, in order for those mistakes not to be repeated.

I dare to say that the only reasonable explanation for our societies' evolution to the newly christened 'tolerant' (but actually un-tolerant) age we are in is that the darkness of this world is beginning to take a firm hold on our planet Earth— just as the Bible predicted.

We have lost far too many of the good qualities that distinguish us as God's creation, then sold our souls and given in to the world's desires and lusts, especially with regard to our fellow human. Whether we agree or disagree, people should be able to talk about practically anything with other people. We are insulted by differing points of view, yet, we are all unique individuals. Isn't it healthy for humankind to respectfully debate matters on which we disagree?

Instead, for fear of offending someone, we now bottle up all of our arguments and keep them close to us, and as a result, our society has become increasingly tense. That rage is palpable in today's world, and it's only growing worse.

Don't get me wrong, the blame is not only placed on cancel culture. We *all* have issues with tolerance, me included. However, it seems today we have far less patience with people in general... even with trivial issues.

Consider anything insignificant, such as internet speed, long traffic lights, cash register line-ups, or being placed on hold. They're all essentially 'first-world' issues, yet they're enough to make us enraged. Society swiftly feels fury at such mere inconveniences.

Is our new social system putting us under so much strain that we're treating each other this way? Yes, it is. How can we distance ourselves from this destructive emotion?

As I'm sure most have seen, there's a meme that questions if you'd rather live in a small cabin in the woods or have a stress filled life in the city. What would you choose? A cabin in the middle of nowhere sounds great. No phone, no internet, no TV. Would life not be so much simpler without the stuff we deal with on a daily basis?

Yes, it would... for about ten minutes, until you realize you must hunt and forage for your food. You'll also need to fetch water from the creek, cut firewood to keep warm, wash your clothing in a bucket, and use an outhouse to go to the bathroom.

I think you get the picture. The grass always seems so much greener... until it's not. Why can't we seem to be happy regardless of our situations?

As society gets more advanced, I believe people are also becoming 'less human'. The result of being less human is that people also tend to care less about each other. It is a sad thing for humanity to realize this, but this is happening right before our eyes. We genuinely only care about our *own* happiness. Period. Us coming first is a very *human* trait.

Even though I am somewhat of an introvert, I do desire to understand how people think. Not to prove them wrong, but I find it important to listen to what they have to say. It's also good to learn *why* they think the way they do. This is how we grow as people in society and learn from each other.

Having said that, I'm not going to lie. It has taken me a long time to improve these abilities. However, my quest to understand a person's perspective has resulted in learning a lot more about them, as well as a better understanding of 'how' and 'why' they feel the way they do about particular topics. Especially when it comes to a subject where I do not necessarily agree with their logic. I tended to jump all over their words in order to get my point across before they could say anything else, but that only worked for me.

Now, I make an honest effort to listen first assuming they know something I don't. It has taught me that if I can keep my emotions in check long enough to hear them out, I'm usually surprised by the point they're trying to make, and, more often than not, that point was not what I had anticipated. What I learnt from them has shocked me several times, and that new information then sparked new ideas.

It boils down to this. I have had to accept the fact that I don't know everything. That was a very humbling revelation to me, but I'm glad it happened. I recognize that there is way more I do not know, than what I do know, and much of the new information offered was something I never considered before. When I allowed that mutual exchange with someone, the experience of listening almost always brought forth fresh information, which frequently transformed the paradigm of my existing viewpoint.

Discussion is critical in order to subject ourselves to different viewpoints... this is why having a debate is crucial. Paradigm shifts occur all the time in our daily lives. How many times has the inclusion of new information impacted your perspective on something?

Here is an example of a paradigm shift. "A blind woman entered a transit bus. A man who was already on the bus noticed the blind woman stepping on to it. As soon as he saw her, he sprung to his feet and ushered the blind woman to his seat."

Would you say, this was a good thing or a bad thing?

This, most of us would agree, was a good thing. We'd think that it was a very thoughtful gesture, a kind thing to do… right?

Well, allow me to present some new information that might change that thought. The man who gave up his seat on the bus to the blind woman was in fact the bus driver. You see, the paradigm completely shifted with that small piece of new information. Giving up his seat really wasn't a good thing after all.

What I'm trying to say is that you shouldn't ignore information just because you might not like the outcome. At the very least, pay attention. It may possibly have the potential to save your life.

So… back to God and religion. When I think back on all my trials over the years, I wish someone had just laid it all out in a simple manner without making the belief in God sound so incredibly complicated and boring. It was impossible for me to make sense of it all, and I honestly needed help to understand what it all meant.

How hard is that? Please, someone, just tell me what I need to know. No one could.

I am not any different than most people. I am totally turned off by religion and somber church services. Religion seems so out there when you don't comprehend any of it, and does its best to chase people away rather than draw them closer to God because of the weird and terrible stuff that goes on inside of it.

But I have to say, one of the biggest detractors within religion, that absolutely rubs me the wrong way, is the outright hypocrisy. It is no wonder religion has such a disastrous reputation. People are discouraged from wanting to know more about God because of paedophile priests and deceitful preachers. Instead of wanting to know more, we run away from the hypocrisy. How can you blame anyone for feeling this way.

To make matters worse, prosperity preachers not only give you false hope, but they also take your money while giving you that false hope. You know the ones, "Send money and we will pray for you and heal your illnesses." Or they say, "Perhaps by giving a little extra this month, your positivity and giving will bless you, and if you continue to support our ministry, you will become wealthy and healthy."

These groups are probably the worst offenders for turning people away, especially after church goers become wise to their counterfeit program. This is not good.

Religions are odd, and they have done so much damage to people's faith in God. It's easy to see why religion has a mostly negative impact on society.

Also, why do religious people constantly come across as weird and strange? This is a difficult thing for me to accept, I mean… can't you all just be cool.

I wish religious people would stop acting as if they were God's children. You know why… because unbelievers can't tell the difference between the deceptive children of God and the sincere ones, so anyone who has a belief in God is grouped into the same category… the religious one.

The last thing I desire is to be lumped into the same category as religion, because even though we might believe in the same God, it's a battle before I even begin to talk since I need to make it clear that my beliefs are not the same as theirs.

Most of us don't realize religion isn't what God is all about. There is a HUGE difference between 'religions', 'religious people' and true 'Christianity'. I never described myself as a religious person and do my best to clarify the difference. How can anyone be blamed for being skeptical of God when we can plainly see what religions stand for?

But wait… hold on a second. Don't throw the baby out with the bathwater. Just because the bathwater is cold and dirty, it does not mean the baby is the same.

In the same way, we throw away God because religions have done such a poor job convincing people of the goodness of God. Religions are like the dirty bathwater, so don't throw away God just because religions have not done God justice. God is amazing, and we absolutely need him in our lives.

When you consider this twisted and chaotic existence, you recognize that this can't possibly be all there is. So, what's the point of it all? Do we only live for a brief time, soaking up as much happiness and joy as we can before passing away?

What about grief, sadness, and suffering? These are also very real aspects of life, although not everyone will have equal amounts of them in their lifetime.

How is this fair? Do we vanish into blackness when our lives are over, or is there something else once we leave this world? How can we be certain?

After so much doubt and false teaching in my life, I was forced to find the answer to these questions myself. My initial conviction was that maybe the overall 'worldly' explanation of our existence might hold some truth.

However, I quickly recognized that, contrary to atheism, we could not have arisen from nothing, nor could this wonderfully designed universe have 'evolved' from disorganization. It is just not possible.

Nevertheless, there is another explanation to our existence that we were all taught some time ago before the rise of the modern era. That historical teaching focused on God and how he created everything. No-one ever questioned the logic of it because everyone in that time read the instruction manual... which explained everything.

The Bible made perfect sense to people until certain scientists and authors began to create books challenging the biblical account of creation, citing it as a myth. Humanity soon snatched up this new explanation for our existence, and after reading its literature, many individuals opted to disbelieve God.

People were no longer compelled to listen to their moral consciences and life suddenly became more liberating when the requirement to follow God was removed. It spread like wildfire.

However, I believe we all have a deep desire to discover if God is real. Many millions, if not billions of people, obviously believe he is very real; and the fact that the majority of them are very intelligent people, should make us all wonder if there is much more to God.

This truth clearly struck me, so I set out to discover why people thought this and what knowledge they possessed that I lacked.

So, I started reading the instruction manual— the Bible.

What a crazy book the Bible is. Yet, it is logical, timely, systematic, and makes perfect sense when your heart is open to reading it.

This book not only explains our beginnings, but it also describes our ending. This is the section to which we should pay particular attention.

Yet, an increasing number of individuals are dismissing the Bible as a literal 'story' created by a group of uneducated peasants. This could not be any further from the truth.

The Bible stories are fascinating, and believe it or not, also full of murder, lying, sin, adultery, and even homosexuality.

Most importantly, however, it's a book filled with the love that God has for us and his simple instructions for living a good life.

As a curious person, the challenge I found most difficult if I had questions about God, was how to find true information that clearly explained the realities of the Bible. I discovered plenty of inaccurate interpretations, and viewpoints, but sorting them out proved to be a significant challenge... and incredibly confusing.

Who was correct? Was it the religion, the speaker, or the internet?

Everyone had their own unique perspective, but the real issue was that the vast majority of religious viewpoints strayed from God's real message.

As a result, I began to study the Bible more carefully, but still needed help to understand what I was reading. And ultimately, I became even more confused because what I understood from reading the Bible did not correspond to the explanation I was listening to or reading about.

So, how else can you approach things? Where do you turn if you're curious about God and want to learn more, because most people find church unappealing?

Believe me, I get it. It is pretty darn intimidating... even as a Christian. I'm not saying that church isn't great, because it REALLY is, but most people simply find it overwhelming and uncomfortable to hang out with 'religious' folks just trying to fit in. You feel like a complete outsider because you have no idea what they are talking about.

I grew up with religious parents and had a basic understanding of what God was all about. Even then, it was weird. But to someone who has never experienced religion, I think it would be not only confusing, but even shocking. Honestly, I get it.

Not knowing where else to turn, you then, in your quest for answers, turn to the TV or go online and someone speaking piques your interest. Great! You start listening more intently, but you soon figure out that they are teaching an advanced lesson for *actual* religious people. Again, the lesson is so over your head that you have no idea what they are talking about, especially if you have never been exposed to this stuff before. How long are you going to stay tuned to that show until you get totally frustrated and switch the channel?

I then thought, how could I get the attention of people who don't necessarily fit into the church mold? Or any mold, for that matter.

I mean, let's face it, in the modern age we live in, if you start talking about God, you are totally brushed off by society. We love our life of sinful behavior. Why would we want to hear about someone named 'God' whom we might have to answer to when we die? That speculation doesn't exactly make God very appealing.

I thought this too. But now that I understand how important it is to believe in God, I decided to try a different approach to grab the attention of folks like me, with a beginner's guide to... what's up with those weirdos who love God?

As a Christian, I feel like an anomaly most of the time. It's becoming difficult to find people who openly want to discuss their beliefs because society, in general, no longer wants to address such questions.

Yet questions are vital, and I want to be able to respond to and answer questions. I believe the error in our thinking is that we don't actually realize how big of deal God is until we know him. It's my desire to help people understand why knowing God should be the number one priority in our lives, and I will explain why this is essential in the chapters ahead.

In today's contemporary culture, I hope to write honestly in a way that speaks loudly to folks like me because this, in my opinion, is required to help people understand the grace of God.

I myself don't fit the stereotype of a bible thumper, and so it was difficult for me to join a church. Unfortunately, I was lost for quite some time, and I don't want you to experience the same fate. In our lives, we don't want to waste any of the precious time we might have left.

I also think the Bible is usually not taught in such

a way that people need to hear it. My former religion did not teach me anything about the Bible.

As a result of my experience, I'm going to attempt to tell you what I have learned by reading, praying, and studying God's word and the world. Some of it will be brutally honest, but I believe that's how I would have liked to hear it. I really don't like it when people try to pacify me by telling me what I want to hear; that's an insult to my intelligence and it does not benefit me in any way. I've learned over time that hearing the truth is the healthiest way to hear things, even if the truth is difficult to hear and often painful to our ego.

However, being truthful does not mean sharing the truth while blaming or shaming someone. It is far more crucial to tell the truth with love and kindness than to save our own pride. Our culture mistakenly believes that pride is the most important aspect of life and that it is important for us to hold our heads high in society. It's not. None of us are perfect. Pride will only lead to more lying.

What do you suppose would happen if someone told you that you were doing a 'wonderful job' at work, and then, you were fired four months later because they weren't truthful about your lousy performance? What would your reaction be if that happened?

I completely appreciate the need for positive reinforcement since we don't have to be nasty to one another, but this constant encouragement, without fault, has gotten to the point of being downright deceptive. When the truth is finally revealed, it is far more painful than the lie, and you will soon recognize that what was said to you was a deception to protect your feelings.

This is not in anyone's best interests. Don't be such sensitive snowflakes. It is fine for us to not be perfect and to be criticized. It pushes us to become better individuals and encourages us to change our poor behavior. This is also affirmed in the Bible.

I also needed to hear the truth about myself, and was fortunate to have a brilliant young man in my life who was completely truthful and honest with me.

I was a hypocrite, and as painful as it was to hear, I needed this man's, and God's, revelations to start to transforming me and my attitude. The truth has quietly humbled me, and I believe that for any of us to think clearly, humility is required. Get over yourself. It's not about us.

Whether or not you've ever considered following God, I pray society doesn't continue to shut your eyes and ears whenever his name is mentioned. I accept that life is crazy and that you may be too distracted to think about anything, especially God. I hear you. This incredibly demanding life shows no signs of slowing down any time soon.

I also understand how tough it is to find quiet moments in life, particularly ones that are peaceful enough to allow you to gather your thoughts. Taking the time to find out the truth about God is, nevertheless, critical.

So how do we move forward?

It's quite simple, really. First thing, ask important questions. Next, answer those questions. Hopefully as you begin to read this book, the answers will begin to emerge because I had the same questions. Most of us have the same questions about life but we don't make the time to answer them right away thinking that we will have time later in life.

Life is short. Death is a guarantee. Don't wait.

My job is to plant a seed. Your job is to open your heart. God's job is to open your eyes. I will be praying for you.

Don't lose hope.

Chapter Two
What's The Diff?

Christianity is the only true and perfect religion...
– Benjamin Rush, Declaration of Independence

Here's the first topic: Religion versus Christianity. What's the difference and why is true Christianity so important?

Think of God's word, the Bible, as a bowl of plain vanilla ice cream. Vanilla is pretty darn tasty all on its own, right?

But in order to sell more of it you will want to make that plain vanilla ice cream more appealing by adding all kinds of flavours like bananas, nuts, sprinkles, chocolate sauce, whipping cream, and of course, a cherry on the top.

Now you have an ice cream sundae. That sounds way more delicious than 'plain ole' vanilla, and chances are good that you would probably sell many more sundaes than bowls of plain vanilla ice cream.

This is similar to religion, in a sense. Even though no two faiths are the same, the foundations on which they have evolved are. Almost every religion begins with God's Word, which is the Bible.

Now, I'd like to believe this is done with good intentions, but in order to accommodate different personal viewpoints in the world, religions then add their own toppings (words/works) to make their beliefs seem more appealing. And because we want to please people, religions tell us what we want to hear, not what we *need* to hear, thereby straying from the Bible's original intent and what God has instructed us.

In simple terms, religions make up their own guidelines that are easier for people to follow rather than using God's rule book, the Bible.

I know this firsthand. It was super easy for me to be a member of a religion because I only went to church when it was convenient for me. If something good was happening that day, I didn't have to miss out on anything. I just didn't go to church. Then, if I happened to feel like I had done something sinful and had guilt to go with it, I would conveniently go to church that week or say some repetitive prayers as penance. I felt like God, and I were all good.

I was very wrong.

Most religions actually recognize that we all fall short of God's goodness and that forgiveness is required. Religions add 'works righteousness' (performing good actions, repetitious prayer, etc.) to their doctrines in order to raise us to the high pedestal that we need to be on in order to be forgiven by God.

According to the religions structure, these good deeds may allow us to reach 'good person' status in that belief; and after we achieve good person status and feel good about ourselves as a result of our good deeds, we believe we have done everything we can to earn God's forgiveness.

Of course, it is much easier for us to live in this world believing that we are in God's good books, having the impression that we are on the correct track toward heaven.

The versatility of religion appeals to us immensely because many modify the original biblical message set out by God to seemingly suit our needs.

We love to embrace the freedom to select a religion in accordance with our individual preferences and choices. Humans can't help but to be drawn to these religious practices invented by man rather than God, since religious ideology does not hold us accountable for our sins. We create a fluffy god to worship who is unconcerned with disobedience to his commands.

It's way easier, but won't conform to what God has rightly determined our needs are.

Religion's main goal is typically not to uphold God's message; rather, it is to attract a sizable following looking for a 'feel good' message. It's no surprise there are huge mega-churches out there with massive followings because it is pleasing to be a part of something that helps us feel good about ourselves.

However, the majority of faiths must add or remove 'rules' from God's word. These principles are referred to as pagan beliefs, which literally means "not of God."

The end result of this type of belief system is almost always related to accumulating more wealth; the only group that genuinely benefits from it are religions. It is no longer about God. It's all about money and notoriety.

Being a follower of a non-biblical religion will not save you… no matter how good *you* believe you are. This is the truth.

For true Christians, the plain vanilla ice cream is good all on its own. That is all that is needed. A true Christian loves God and loves and trusts His Son Jesus.

Christians understand that Jesus came to pay the ultimate price for our sins. They rely solely on the Bible for instruction, and live according to what God has spoken in the Bible.

Christians who believe, love, and trust in Jesus, God's son, can be confident that they will go to heaven.

Honestly, that's all that's needed; no good works, no good deeds, and no repetitive prayers. It's really very simple. ***Seek the plain vanilla ice cream.***

Chapter Three

Fake News

Education is useless without the Bible.
– Daniel Webster, early American politician

When we are faced with adversity in life, this BIG question comes to mind. What evidence do we have that there is a God?

It's a simple question to answer. Take a look around. God's handiwork can be found all throughout the world. I'll explain how I came to this conclusion.

Consider the spinning ball we live on and all that surrounds it. How could this planet be so perfectly balanced for life to exist? Let's set aside everything else we assume we know for a moment and simply talk about the planet Earth.

Have you ever considered all the factors that would have had to come together for humans to be able to exist on this planet? Normally, we wouldn't have any reason to ask this question. We have always known the earth. It's here, it's in good working order, and the days just keep ticking by. Rarely are we encouraged to understand more about why or how we arrived here.

Humanity believes it has found answers to all of life's difficult problems, yet fresh knowledge is always being uncovered. We hear about discoveries on occasion, so we read the headlines and occasionally go further into the articles, however, the majority of readers do not read the complete text and have hardly scratched the surface on any given topic.

I do this all the time because I believe I grasp what they are saying after reading the first few lines. This is all the information we want because we just don't have time for more in our hurried lives.

Furthermore, we are assaulted with information on a daily basis, making it difficult to keep current. As a result, rather than digging further into the facts, people turn to experts to explain what's going on.

Yet, what I found very interesting is that we don't often question the outcomes of experts. Why is that? I suppose we trust that the experts know what they are doing. Fair enough, they have had many years of schooling and practice to determine these things and we haven't.

But what we are told doesn't always make sense, such as the complicated evolutionary explanation for the sun's existence. Scientists argue that waves of energy travelling across space pulled clouds of particles together, which ultimately collapsed in on themselves due to gravity. After that, the particles had to start spinning, causing the gas clouds to flatten out like a pancake. The material in the middle of this spinning pancake then clumped together to create a form of protostar, which eventually became the sun.

We appear to be mystified by the science because the process is so complex. Confusion appears to be a path to science's credibility.

However, there is a problem. Nothing can be replicated by a person or a machine from millions or billions of years ago; or even tens of thousands of years ago. It is impossible to repeat the beginning of the universe to verify that it was as the experts say it was. Humans cannot prove anything.

Science often uses influenced perceptions with parts of the observation missing or left out; not the entire insight. It seems like the impact of this influence becomes a belief of the scientist by the time they have completed their education.

Having a belief is not the job of a scientist. A scientist's goal should be to show data that can be replicated over and over in order to demonstrate that the information presented is accurate and based on facts. This is real science.

But, because the science is structured in this particular way, most scientists have a view that is only inside the lenses of their binoculars. Unfortunately, in today's culture, that view has become normalized. In part because we no longer ask questions about the facts, but I also believe we are tired of asking questions.

The same narrative has been told for so long that we believe it to be factual without question.

This is not the correct way to consider such important science. There is so much more to investigate and question because when you break things down and use critical thinking, much of what we've been told makes absolutely no sense.

Yet, within the field of science, the vast majority of us do not want to 'rock the boat.' We tend to blindly trust the information from the professionals without requiring any further verification.

Consider the methods used and the conclusions drawn by employing those methods. How did the researchers arrive at their conclusions? Was it strictly through technical analysis or did they use critical thinking as well? Was it possible for scientists to confirm that their method of dating artifacts was one hundred percent accurate?

We assume they provide us with absolute certainty, but clearly, they can't for these analyses because there is no basis for comparison.

Since all of the facts are not available, it's insane to believe that the prevalent evolutionary theory is right. It can't be. And, in reality, all of the facts will never be available.

If you read scientific articles closely, you'll notice that experts admit this over and over again. They use terms such as, 'probably,' 'likely,' 'presumably,' 'maybe,' 'possibly,' 'we believe,' 'our conclusion,' and so on.

That's fantastic, but please don't present your information as factual. This is extremely deceptive.

Despite popular belief, because technological advances have made leaps and bounds in recent years, science frequently sides with opposition to evolutionary claims. I think the subject of where we came from is relevant enough to elicit further inquiries about it because, in terms of our origins, science has not been able to prove anything.

But I get it. We are tired of hearing the skeptics. It is easier to agree with the narrative of the majority and not ask questions.

In light of not knowing the past for certain, these facts we do know.

We are the third planet that spins around a fiery hot sun, and that fiery hot sun is 93 million miles away.

Consider that for a moment. Ninety-three million miles, and yet, the sun is just far enough away to perfectly ripen our tomatoes. If there was a small change in distance either way, we would not be here, nor would our tomatoes. Ninety-two million miles away, we would fry. Ninety-four million miles away, we would freeze. How unbelievable is that?

But this is only one incredible variable. There are many more.

Not only is our earth the perfect distance away from the sun, but it is also the perfect size. What great randomness… lucky us!

Now, consider the other planets in our solar

system spinning at correct speeds. Again, not too fast and not too slow. Not only do they spin at the ideal speeds, but these planets are also in the perfect orbits, which is needed for all of this to work in sync… and amazingly, it all works flawlessly.

These planets are not just there for show, either. Every planet in our solar system plays an important role in keeping the earth and everything else up there in order. Without the planets doing what they do, there would be certain chaos and *we* wouldn't be here.

But let's move on.

What about the Earth's atmosphere? It is a crazy mix of approximately seventy-eight percent nitrogen and twenty-one percent oxygen, including trace amounts of water, argon, carbon dioxide, and other gases thrown in for good measure.

There is no other planet in our solar system with a free-flowing atmosphere. Free air is also vital to one of the other unique features of the Earth: Life. And as far as we know, we are the only planet with any proven 'life'.

Earth's journey to this point has not been easy. A slew of seemingly improbable circumstances had to have aligned for life to exist. What are the odds these events actually happened at random?

At this stage in evolution, we have a sun that is ninety-three million miles away and an atmosphere that contains the perfect combination of extremely complex components essential for human life. These are already incredible odds for the first stages of life, and keep in mind that the theory of our origins provides no other explanation than random chance.

But, for the sake of argument, let's just pretend that these events occurred as they claimed. What else can we learn about this planet that will stimulate our curiosity?

Perhaps think about the unique magnetic field generated in the earth's outer core and lying 1800 miles beneath the surface. The churning metals in earth's core function as a huge generator, propelling an electromagnetic field, tens of thousands of kilometres into space and shielding us from the cosmic rays and solar wind.

Why is this important? Because without it, our ozone layer would be stripped away and leave us unprotected from UV rays. If it was not present, there would be no humans.

It is also the earth's key to holding water on our planet. Without water, nothing survives. Not humans, not animals, nor plants. No water, no air, no life.

Our complex magnetic field is specifically designed to protect us from being harmed by all of the other forces. This is not possible by chance due to the odds being inconceivable.

Also, examine our moon. Admiring the full moon in the night sky is one of my favourite things to do. It's quite amazing, especially if you've had the opportunity to see it through a telescope. But the moon isn't just there to provide a 'bright light' during our dark nights. The earth could slow down to the point where it wobbles out of control if the moon's gravitational influence is removed.

Scientists believe the moon was formed when a 'porto-planet' around the size of Mars collided with the Earth 4.5 billion years ago (this is a guess, not a fact). The moon was then formed from the material left behind after the impact.

However, according to experts, it would have had to develop to the exact same size as it is now in order to perform as it does; otherwise, the moon would not be able to assist the Earth in any way.

Consider how difficult this process would have been. And when you consider how magnificent the moon is and how it impacts the functionality of our planet, what are the chances of this happening at random? Honestly?

Many other planets play significant roles as well. Jupiter, because of it's enormous size, has a super strong gravitational pull, so instead of impacting the earth, meteors are instead attracted to this planet often saving us from disaster.

Could you imagine looking up every two minutes to see whether a meteor was about to strike the earth? Well, because of Jupiter, we don't have to.

Here's a recap: Our planet, Earth, *just happens* to be the perfect distance from the sun. Then, all of the other planets in our solar system *just happen* to all be precisely coordinated, which is absolutely necessary to control our ride here on earth. Then, we *just happen* to have an atmosphere on Earth that *just happens* to be the perfect combination of all of the elements and gases needed to provide us with the free air we require as humans. Then, we *just happen* to have a magnetic field for solar protection and water, and a moon that *just happens* to keep us in orbital check.

In this case, use your critical thinking skills. Every single one of these actions is anything but a random chain of events, but they are all necessary for us to be here. They are very, very complicated.

How many billions of years do you suppose it would have taken for just these factors to come together at random?

This is where we should take a big step back and contemplate the vast complexity of the many factors that had to be taken into consideration in order for the ball which we are presently inhabiting to be functional enough to host life. All we can really say is, "I haven't thought about it that much..."

I know. I didn't either, until now.

Even with our ability as humans to cheat, random chance never seems to work. So what are the odds of it working within the harsh conditions of the universe? Well I can tell you... not very likely.

Here's what a well-known British mathematician and close friend of atheist Stephen H. had to say about it.

The scientist calculated the probability of the

initial entropy conditions being random to be in the neighbourhood of 10 to the 123rd power. This is the number 10 with 123 zeros after it. Try writing it, because the number is so huge, we can't even say it. Odds of less than 1 to the 50th power is equal to 'zero probability' and the number stated by the scientist is more than a trillion trillion trillion times *less* probable than that.

The 'accidental' or 'coincidental' creation of our universe is simply impossible, after all, we are not talking about a single random event. We're talking about winning the jackpot over and over again, well beyond what chance could possibly account for.

To put this another way, believing that evolution happened by chance requires far more faith than believing that an all-powerful God created the universe.

Something I once read put it this way. Concentrate on what is being conveyed in this great analogy. "If there were two million people playing a game of dice together... but not with regular playing dice. These dice each had a trillion sides on them. And in the game the two million players roll the dice at the same time."

Here's the question: "What is the chance that the two million players who roll the dice with a trillion sides on it, at the exact same time, come up with the exact same number?"

Easy answer. Zero. Absolutely and emphatically, ZERO chance.

If you use this comparison to represent all of the factors that would have had to come together for evolution to produce the beautiful planet we live on, it's clear that it's not conceivable. Even if scientists believe it took millions or billions of years for our planet to evolve into the world we know today, there is simply not enough time to form an environment suitable for life as we know it.

So, why do we have such faith in scientists' analogies?

Great question… but it gets better.

Until now, I've only talked about evolutionists' theories on how the world and galaxy formed, but let's take a look at what evolutionists believe happened next.

We'll give evolutionists the benefit of the doubt for the following challenge.

Let's assume that after the formation of the earth, we now had a suitable environment on earth for habitation. So, what's next?

Take another look around; what do you see?

Rivers, oceans, plants, trees, rich soil and sand, minerals, elements, and rocks. This is the environment in which things may grow and continue to flourish. With four seasons of rain, wind, sun, and snow, our ecosystem is amazingly and meticulously balanced. Cloud cover, salt water in the ocean, fresh water in the lakes, and streams to drink are all abundant and here to help us to survive.

So how did this all come together? Are we not fortunate to live on a planet that functions with the precision of a clock? Is it random chance once again?

For as long as the earth has existed, rivers and streams have flowed into the oceans. Why then, have we never experienced a rise in the oceans because of it? That's a lot of water constantly flowing into the ocean. How could evaporation and weather cycles, among everything else, have randomly evolved and become so perfect.

Is it maybe possible that our planet simply takes care of itself? After all, these processes on Earth operate like a well-tuned engine.

The second law of thermodynamics, on the other hand, asserts that "order produces chaos," rather than the other way around. The net entropy (degree of disorder) of any isolated or closed system will always rise as time passes (or at least stay the same). If left unchecked, chaos will grow over time. Energy dissipates, and systems disintegrate.

How did the world begin in chaos and end up in such a remarkable and magnificent state of order? Because, according to the evolutionary theory, things did not begin with order.

Scientists are still trying to figure out how humanity moved from chaos to order. This is when common sense should really come into the equation.

Other than a good bottle of wine or fine whiskey, things generally do not get better with age or time. The scientific community has yet to produce any hard evidence to back up their theories, and because they do not have any credible facts, scientists try to support their beliefs by using the addition of more time to their timeline.

Don't you find that just a little suspicious? There isn't a single scientist who supports evolution that can provide any real evidence to back it up.

Of course, they can't. They literally don't have any information to give.

Evolutionists, according to scientists, apparently know everything there is to know about the missing link. Critics, on the other hand, have asserted that scientists know all there is to know about the missing link, except that the 'missing link' is genuinely missing.

And yet, even more scientists claim that there are gaps in the fossil record where no transitional forms exist. They point out that Darwin's hypothesis and the fossil record are clearly at odds, and that there are palaeontologists who also oppose Darwin's theory. It isn't nearly as solid a hypothesis as evolutionists makes it out to be. Even Darwin acknowledged that his hypothesis had flaws.

So, as scientists suggest, did evolution begin with a single cell?

A Cambridge astronomer, one of the most important scientific minds of the twentieth century and a well-respected leader in his profession, wrote about the random emergence of even the simplest form of a cell.

He described the random chance of cell

development, based on his research, like this: "The random emergence of a single cell is comparable to the likelihood of a tornado blowing through a junkyard and hurling everything up in the air. Then, as the debris lands on the ground, it produces a Boeing 747 with all of its systems in perfect working order."

These are simply ridiculous odds and completely unattainable. We are all aware of the devastation of a tornado. It completely destroys rather than creates perfection. Besides, we can't even win the lottery with a one-in-a-million chance, so how could evolution have happened on purpose and so many times?

But what the heck... let's throw even more complicated systems into this mix to expose the misrepresentation of what we've been told.

Plant life also exists on this planet.

What was the origin of the very first seed and with millions of distinct plants, how do we explain the earth's plant life? Why would something as insignificant as a seed exist in the cosmos at all?

Assume that the climate on Earth was suited for plant life, even if just by coincidence. Why would anything need to grow? Shouldn't the Earth have remained the same as the rest of our solar system's planets, barren, and incapable of supporting life? What makes the Earth unique?

But, for the sake of argument, let us continue to give evolutionists the benefit of the doubt.

Assume that one seed appeared out of nowhere at

random. After the initial seed landed and miraculously germinated, how did we end up having millions of plant kinds here on Earth? Any journey through the universe, I imagine, would have been a harsh environment for a seed. Not much survives in the cosmos, never mind a bunch of fragile seeds.

How can we explain the origins of the millions of distinct seeds? Could the answer be evolution once more?

Another consideration: As far as we know, no other planet has a viable growth environment, so it's unlikely that a seed would have originated there. Seeds, in particular, would have had to adapt to an entirely different environment from which they came from.

Isn't it strange that seeds appeared on Earth at random? And, when you consider how well-suited these plants are for us to consume, nourish our bodies, and feed the animals that help nourish us, don't you think they might be a miracle?

Furthermore, these plants have the right balance of nutrients, fibres, vitamins, and minerals that people and animals require.

Again, this is a complicated synopsis. It's a lot to consider, I know.

However, they say it's random chance, a coincidence, and I suppose if you hear that sentence enough times you might accept it. But, in my opinion, the evidence strongly suggests that the plants were created specifically for mankind to survive.

What would be the point of the Earth if people weren't here to enjoy all of its wonderful features? Would planet Earth have been created if it hadn't been for us humans?

There are countless wonders within this complex system that are necessary to provide humanity with an ideal environment. Experts have an untold amount of questions yet to answer because more show up every time they discover something new.

Yet, scientists believe that the emergence of the first living organism from a plant cell was the next step on our path to life.

Well, how did this come to be and why would any single one of these plant cells change into an animal in the first place? Natural selection seems to be the only answer scientists have, although it appears to be an excuse for a lot of things.

Maybe... just thinking outside the box in the spirit of an evolutionist's rational on plant life: Did living animals evolve because plants required something to consume them now that there were plants on the planet? Remember that it all had to start with a single random cell. We don't know how that cell appeared in the first place, according to scientists, but they argue that a single cell was the most probable source of life.

They don't have any other choice than to defend the presence of the cell.

Think about what had to happen to get to this point alone... randomly to boot. Even if there was rock solid proof of an evolutionary beginning, how long did it take for the Earth to arrive at this point? Or perhaps, does the entire theory seem so far-fetched that this narrative is more likely to be unbelievable?

I'd put my money on the second explanation because when you combine many of the evolutionists statements together, they make no logical sense. Every phase of the process had to have been based on an unfathomable random chance.

However, in reality, science does not operate on the premise of miraculous random chance, and no matter how many times you ask, "Why, why, why, why, why, why," there is no way to support any of the claims. We are again bewildered by scientists elaborate explanations.

Nonetheless, let's continue and examine the animals of the planet.

We have determined that evolutionary scientists claim everything we know has manifested from a single cell, and from that single cell, microorganisms then developed. From that micro-organism, came algae, then plants, fish, land animals, and finally, us humans. But let's break this down a bit further.

Contemplate all of the living things in our world, and the infinite variety of them. Animals, both wild and domesticated, birds, reptiles, insects, fish, mammals, microbes, and algae are all present.

According to scientists, there are between 5.3 million and 1 trillion species on the planet. We can't even be sure of the precise number of species on this planet since there are many that we have not yet discovered.

Imagine going to the bank and inquiring about the balance of your account and the teller responds with, "I'm not exactly sure, but somewhere between $5.30 and $1,000,000,000 dollars."

According to scientific consensus, 81% of the earth's species remain unknown to us, and we are still a long way from knowing them all. To this day, just 14% of land animals and 9% of aquatic creatures have ever been catalogued by scientists. And, if all of the millions of species that make up today's world, according to evolutionists, had to develop into the perfect beings that they are, there must have been numerous mutations and mistakes along the way. In spite of those mutations, all we observe today are fully flawless beings, whether they are organisms, plants, animals, or us.

Well, scientists say it all started 3.8 billion years ago... or maybe 3.5 billion years... or was it 2.15 billion years ago? Evolutionists are excellent guessers, but humanity really doesn't have a clue.

Despite being encouraged to trust that we have it all figured out, there is zero factual evidence to verify these assumptions. In truth, we have no idea about a great many things.

Insects. In everyday life we take insects for granted. They are, nonetheless, a very crucial component of existence as you may have guessed, even the unpleasant ones. Insects are busy little machines that never stop working to ensure that our world runs smoothly... we can't survive without them.

Did you know that insects like the honeybee labour around the globe to ensure our survival?

The bee is a fascinating bug. Honeybees are needed by the earth to pollinate plants in order for crops to recover each year and produce their fruits. We would not be able to sustain our food supply or the food source of the animals that feed us if bees were not present. Around three-quarters of the world's plants require pollination for reproduction.

If bees become extinct, it is projected that our food supply would be depleted very quickly. We'd only be able to survive for around four years. If you think about it, that's pretty terrifying.

How can you best describe this one tiny insect that is precisely designed to perform a key role on the planet?

To be honest, I believe it would take far longer than 3.8 billion years for the honeybee to reach its current perfection. Without the honeybees, we would not be able to exist in this world. How can anyone say that a little creature such as a bee could have developed into an absolutely perfect instrument for human survival out of supposed 'chaos'?

Consider the bee's complex life cycle, reproductive system, and sensory characteristics. What makes you think an insect like this would emerge from thin air in the first place? What would be the point of it?

Plus, after all that this tiny insect does for us, the bee gives us something extra. Natural honey is both delicious and healthy for us.

Is it by chance?

That is an excellent question. I'm not sure I can answer that question, and I'm guessing evolutionists can't either, but the bee appears to have been created specifically for the planet Earth and its people. Who'd have guessed that this small insect was designed with a specific purpose in mind? Go figure.

Insects are absolutely essential workers, not just for preserving life on Earth, but also for keeping a harmonious balance. Many insects actually prevent aphids and other crop-damaging pests from invading our crops.

How about those gorgeous ladybugs and dragonflies? They, like every other living thing on the planet, have occupations. Both are credited for consuming the larvae of pesky insects before they have a chance to take over the planet. If that takeover occured, we humans would find it unbearable to be outside.

Think of world where we are continuously bitten by flying insects that transmit dangerous diseases. It's a good thing they are here for us because without insects, humans wouldn't last very long.

Consider the simple earthworm. Worms are

commonly thought of as good bait for trout fishing. Ahh, but it has a bigger job to do. Its poop improves the PH of the soil, allowing our plants to grow robust and healthy. Worms also wriggle through the dirt, leaving behind tiny tunnels that aerate the soil, allowing irrigation to reach the roots of the plants more readily. As you can see, the little earthworm performs a critical role that you've probably never considered.

Everything has a purpose. Absolutely everything. All of these things I have described are perfect. They always have been.

I am wondering if you are seeing this. Please tell me you are at least starting to see the fable we have been taught to believe. No, these things are NOT still evolving. They have no reason to evolve further. They do adapt, however. Creatures adapt to their environment depending on their surroundings and climate, just like humans do.

Another misconception that is very important to understand is the difference between 'evolution' and 'adaptation'.

Evolution requires something to change from 'it's kind' to 'another kind'. Like a dog turning into a turkey.

Adaptation, on the other hand, is the fine tuning of a species to help it manage its specific environment. We see plenty of adaptation on the earth, such as a dog that lives in cold weather versus a dog that lives in a warmer climate. A cold-weather dog will have different fur than a dog that lives in a warmer climate... but it's still a dog.

Darwin's 'famous finches' grew different beaks in order to adapt to their environment. But they were still finches. Darwin deceivingly classified the change in their beaks as evolution. This is NOT evolution, it's adaptation.

Then there are the humans. Please explain to me how one single random cell, among everything else that supposedly evolved from it, also randomly created the incredibly complex system that we call our body?

What do you believe came first, whether in a human or a creature? The heart perhaps, because it's the perfect pump and so very complicated.

You say, "OK, sure, it was the heart."

So why, then, did the heart develop first if we did not yet have any blood vessels to carry the blood?

You then say, "Ok, ok... I suppose you are right. I didn't actually think about that. Well, maybe it was blood and blood vessels that evolved first."

But then you must ask, "Why was there blood?"

Blood is an incredibly intricate balance of plasma, platelets, white blood cells, and red blood cells. How did blood evolve? And again, for what purpose?

Hmmm, you say, "OK, ok, ok. Maybe the lungs were first? Without them no life, right? We must have had lungs in order to breathe the air to keep us alive. When we stop breathing, we die."

But why did lungs develop first if there wasn't a heart, blood or blood vessels to carry the blood or oxygen? And where did the nutrients that travel within the bloodstream, go? Anybody?

How about our amazing eyes? The eye is a perfect combination of a lens, pupil, cornea, sclera, macula, retina, vitreous, eyelashes and eyelids, with an optic nerve that connects to the brain. That optic nerve sends what you are seeing to your brain and converts it to our thoughts in milliseconds. How complicated is that? Like wow!

The incredible eye also has over 126 million light-sensitive cells. It is so intricate and so delicate. Why would an eye even begin to evolve? And how did we have vision before the eye evolved enough to see? How did we live without sight?

I know. I can't explain these questions either.

Perhaps we just started as a blob of a stomach that 'blobbed' its way around because it was hungry. Do you think it had hands or legs? Without limbs, how did we forage, eat, or move?

Or did our stomach blob simply suck up bacteria from the ground until we were strong enough to evolve other parts of our body, such as ears, eyes, nose, mouth, skin, hair, tongue, teeth, etc.? What do you think?

Oh no, I forgot. Scientists say the skin was actually

first because it derived from ancient sponges.

Skin had to have grown first in order to encapsulate the organs that weren't there yet. But why would an organ or skin evolve if there was no such thing as a human, or creature, that needed them? Scientists' explanations make absolutely no sense. The chicken and the egg argument on steroids.

Ahh, but I saved the best for last. The brain. It is composed of three main parts, all with different purposes. The brain consumes twenty percent of the body's oxygen and blood, and contains approximately one hundred billion neurons.

Did you also know that the information going from your arms and legs to your brain travels between 150-260 miles per hour and generates enough power to operate a 20-watt light bulb?

Our amazing 'thinker' is made up of sixty percent fat, with a high-water content, as well as many small blood vessels and soft tissues. Not only does our brain enable us to think, learn, create, taste, and feel emotions, but our brain also enables us to control every breath, bodily function, heartbeat, blink of our eye, and has an unlimited storage capacity. Literally, we don't even need to 'think' about it. It all happens without any effort.

The brain is a miraculous bodily structure that a famous scientist once referred to as, "The most complex thing we have yet discovered in our universe."

Think for a moment about how the brain works.

Our thoughts, our feelings, our moods, reasoning, how we feel compassion. What about our ability to communicate with gestures and speech.

It is not often we put our miraculous brain in context. It is part of our body and because everyone else has one as well, we don't think about what it actually does.

But when you look closely at what your brain is, you must be in awe of it. We are a pretty amazing creation and it would be very easy to go on and on with all the other complicated organs that work effortlessly and in perfect harmony inside of our body, but I think you get the picture.

Each separate body part is completely different from each other, and utterly complicated. We take for granted all the incredible perfection that they are. Isn't it amazing how these parts all work together (within us) to provide 'us humans' with everything we need for life, and a pretty good life at that.

How can anyone believe that all of this happened by 'random chance,' as evolutionists and scientists insist it did? It's not possible.

As intelligent humans, we cannot even create our bodies' simplest organ from scratch with all the advanced technology we have at our disposal without using the DNA of an existing person.

So yeah, I'm sure it all happened randomly. That IS possible, right?

The obvious conclusion is that the earth's animals,

creatures, and humans were perfectly made from the beginning of the earth's creation. People only require a small amount of adaptation to our different environments, much the same as animals, plants, and insects.

Perfection is seen everywhere. In our universe, the sun, planets, the earth, single cells, plants, creatures, and, of course, us humans. We are designed, balanced, and in perfect working order. Do any of these things continue to evolve? Nope, they don't. Everything that we know is already perfect, except for a few anomalies, which can be expected. The Earth is indescribable.

It's a good thing we didn't end up on Venus next door.

I am not a scientist by any means, nor do I claim to be one. I also did not use any unusual methods of computation to arrive at this result. I've merely looked at the evidence available from the scientific community as well as historical texts. I didn't anticipate the evidence to be so overwhelming in favour of creation. Simple common sense is all that is essential in the analogy of life.

Before researching this book, I had no idea how improbable the evolution hypothesis was. Do yourself a favour and exercise your critical thinking skills to examine the data that is available to you.

I understand how difficult it is. I understand you are strapped for time. But, when it comes down to it, and when you think about it, evolution does seem rather ridiculous, doesn't it?

God created us 'good to go', and out of all the theories out there, Creation makes the most sense of all.

Time to take the blinders off, my friends. ***We have been seriously duped.***

Chapter Four
The Origin Of The Lies

"Where were you when I laid the foundation of the earth? Tell me, if you have understanding."
Job 38:4

I have a favourite street preacher I watch online all the time named Ray Comfort, and he uses this analogy when he interviews people on the street. He asks them, "How do you know that a building you can see was built?"

Most people who he asks this question to, reply with, "That's simple, it had a builder."

They're right. A building cannot be built without a builder.

So, when you ask, "How do you know the earth was designed," the answer is simple.

Look at the world. It is obviously created. The fact that it is here, and we are here, living and breathing with this incredible body, is unfathomable, and utterly impossible without a builder (God). There is zero chance of this world randomly happening without a creator.

However, some of you might say, "Good point, but I still believe the scientists. All we need is more time to find all the answers."

Yet the misleading rhetoric of evolution could go on forever with scientists continually dropping enough crumbs of information to keep us believing that they are undoubtedly correct.

My question is, "Why is it so difficult for us to believe that we have a God Creator?"

That's a good question. But the real question is, "When did we begin to believe in evolution as a cause of our existence?"

Most historical documents would say that the belief in evolution started as far back as the 1700's. However, it wasn't until around 1859 when the 'spark' really ignited for this theory.

This was the year that Charles Darwin's book *'The Origin of the Species'* was first published. Darwin was speculating on the modern theory of evolution. Evolution was already somewhat of a theory at that time and was being used as an alternative method to explain the beginning of life instead of using God as the original source.

At that time in his life, Darwin was falling away from his religious beliefs. He was troubled because he started to reason within himself that there must be an explanation to describe life other than God. This propelled Darwin to look outside of the box, as many scientists will naturally do, but Darwin became obsessed with developing his theory.

However, after much work, his theory was never proven. Charles Darwin then hoped that scientists in the future would be able to prove his theory. But as technology becomes better, it's backfired.

Science has become extremely advanced since the time of Darwin's era, and yet, as the equipment for analysis becomes better and better, scientists are still unable to perfectly fit the projected timeline for evolution into the timeline they have predicted for the age of the earth.

As a result of this dilemma, evolutionists have quietly increased the amount of time they claim the Earth has been around for.

But there's a problem.

Because science is becoming more accurate all the time, scientists have also determined that there is a 'hard limit' to the amount of time available for their evolution theory. And by using advanced scientific methods of calculation, that limit of time has already been pushed to the edge. There is simply not enough time and they have run out of 'millions of years' to add to the timeline. The result is that there is no way for the scientists to fit into the timeline all the necessary processes. Life is far too complex for that short window of time.

So now, we hear reports of governments and scientists attempting to explore Mars, hoping to find some sign of life. Anything. But this is yet another attempt to explain how life on earth began.

If scientists can indeed prove that Earth perhaps started with biology from Mars or another planet, the timeline they have predicted now becomes more plausible. They are grasping at straws to prove an unprovable theory.

Regardless of evolutionists inability to factually determine the timeline, Darwin's literature is quite amazing.

He said (in a letter to J. Fordyce May, 1879): "In my most extreme fluctuations, I have never been an atheist in the sense of denying the existence of a God. — I think that generally (and more and more so, as I grow older), but not always, that an agnostic (a person who believes nothing is known of God) would be the most correct description of my state of mind."

Although he thought of religion as a tribal survival strategy, Darwin still truly believed that God was the ultimate lawgiver and later said that he was convinced of the existence of God being the 'first cause' of life.

I find it fascinating how we never hear of Darwin's theistic and then agnostic views in the theory of evolution. Darwin deserved to be called an agnostic, not an atheist, at this midpoint in his life.

However, his views were always in flux, and he continued to explore more doubts without forming any fixed opinions on certain religious matters.

He went as far as saying (1887): "Science has nothing to do with Christ, except insofar as the habit of scientific research makes a man cautious in admitting evidence. For myself, I do not believe that there ever has been any revelation. As for a future life, every man must judge for himself between conflicting vague probabilities."

You see, Darwin was also a man with many doubts, much like most of us now, although I don't think he ever completely denied there being a God.

In a letter to a correspondent at the University of Utrecht in 1873, Darwin was still sounding agnostic, saying: "I may say that the impossibility of conceiving that this grand and wonderous universe, with our conscious selves, arose through chance, seems to me the chief argument for the existence of God; but whether this is an argument of real value, I have never been able to decide. I am aware that if we admit a first cause, the mind still craves to know whence it came from and how it arose. Nor can I overlook the difficulty from the immense amount of suffering through the world. I am, also, induced to defer to a certain extent, to the judgment of many able men who have fully believed in God; but here again I see how poor an argument this is. The safest conclusion seems to me to be that the whole subject is beyond the scope of man's intellect; but man can do his duty."

Another fact that is not so readily known about Charles Darwin is that he lost three of his ten children, and before that, he had also lost his mother at the age of eight.

Of the deaths, the one that impacted him the most, was the loss of his daughter at age nine. As a result of that tragedy, he struggled with growing scepticism toward God. He was obviously mad at God. Fair enough.

It is true that when tragedy strikes in our lives, most of the time, we will stray further away from God. We are naturally upset with God for the painful tragedies we experience. And then, the more we stray from God, the more we doubt. As human beings, we already struggle daily with doubt. Life is not easy.

The pain of loss has happened many times in my life. When life is difficult, we become discouraged.

We then think... where is God? I prayed and nothing happened. Why is this happening to me? Why is God not answering my prayers?

Likewise, when things are going reasonably well, we also forget about God. When things are fine, we don't need Him in our lives...until they're not fine. It seems that we only reach out to God when we are faced with a tragedy or the impending mortality of ourselves or someone we love. Sometimes, in our anger, because of a tragedy that has happened to us, we 'curse' God instead of praying to him.

Regardless of whether it is fury or faith, any emotion toward God is good, especially if it causes you to question and think of more than your mere life.

Unlike us, God is NOT a fragile flower. He knows very well what we are going through and is sincerely waiting for us to seek him. Whether you are doing well or suffering, ask God to show up in your life.

Back to Darwin. In 1870, over one hundred and fifty years ago, Charles Darwin again published another book arguing for the theory of evolution for the human species. This was among his many publications.

'*The Descent of Man*', specifically dealt with Darwin's theory of sexual selection and how evolution may have derived from animal species. But this book was without any real factual proof and depended once again on the concept of 'natural selection' for an explanation. Of course it did.

Darwin then died in 1882 and, unfortunately, has become one of the most influential people in history. But before he died, Charles Darwin said this (1872): "Great is the power of steady misrepresentation…"

That's a powerful statement and powerful misrepresentation is still being used today.

Many years after Darwin died, in 1952, a new method of dating archaeological findings was developed. This new 'radiometric' dating method was exciting, and even more scientists then took up Darwin's cause.

Almost all the outcomes were based on 'modeling' and 'probability' in order to age sedimentary rock; probability through the likelihood of mathematical equations, not factual outcomes.

However, with the eruption of Mount St. Helen's on May 18th, 1980, tangible evidence to factually debunk this method of dating was suddenly available. Now geologists had actual documented evidence of sedimentary rock layers that were created in mere hours, rather than assuming those layers took millions of years.

Scientists dated a ten-year-old rock from the eruption at Mount St. Helens to be 350,000 years old using radiometric dating. Their estimate is only off by 349,990 years. That's close enough... I suppose.

Unlike evolution, the data gathered from the eruption of Mount St. Helen's is not based on probability. This data has not only been studied, recorded, and documented, but it also has been witnessed. Real facts.

Events during the eruption, such as pyroclastic flows, mudflows, airfalls, and stream water during major volcanic events, all contribute to creating these rapid layers. These deposits include 'fine pumice ash laminae beds' from just one millimetre thick to more than one metre thick, with each deposit representing just a few seconds to several minutes of accumulation.

During the evening of June 12, 1980, a stratified deposit, twenty-five feet deep, occurred in just three hours. Coarse and fine sediment were separated into distinct strata from a slurry moving at freeway speeds.

Other things happened as well. On the Toutle River in Washington State, it was witnessed that rapid erosion resembling canyons on a 1/40th scale of the Grand Canyon had occurred.

In the same area, Step Canyon and Loowit Canyon on the north flank of the volcano have bedrock that has been eroded up to six hundred feet deep in a very short period of time. This was the effect of a thick snowpack suddenly becoming a mudflow. Obviously, this is not on the exact same scale as the Grand Canyon, but it certainly proves that this type of deposit and erosion is possible in a short period of time, and that it does not take 'millions' of years.

Did you know, the eruption also showed that petrification of wood happens rapidly in the right conditions. It is caused by individual trees, or entire forests, being deeply buried beneath volcanic ash containing silica. Then hot, 'water-borne' silica gets forced into the wood and also surrounds it, thereby turning it to stone. This process can be easily duplicated in a laboratory.

So, how can anyone, with absolute certainty, determine the age of sedimentary rock? We cannot, and Mt. St. Helen's factually proves this.

Many things happened as a result of the eruption. This mountain not only lost 400 metres of elevation, but sadly, fifty-seven lives were also lost.

Most importantly, however, we now had proof of

the incorrect assumptions that were made regarding the earth's geology. What else could we have possibly wrongly assumed?

More progression towards atheism occurred in 1967, when a court in Arkansas ruled that not being able to teach evolution was unconstitutional. After that time, more and more states ruled in evolution's favour, and things accelerated very quickly from there.

Until Darwin's scientific theories became widely accepted, the Biblical Genesis creation narrative was generally taught as the origin of the universe and life. Now, rarely do you hear of anyone teaching creation outside of a church setting, mostly because it is not allowed.

The push towards atheism escalated once again in November of 1974, when in Ethiopia, archaeologists discovered a few small bones of our now famous museum chimp, Lucy.

Only six of these bone fragments represented head or facial bones, with no hand or foot bones found. But incredibly, from those very few head bones, scientists somehow determined that Lucy had a skull like a human and, of course, that she had walked upright.

This was the lie that changed everything in 1979, when '**Time**' magazine declared Lucy as a front-page celebrity. She was touted as the first representation of a 'hominid' that walked upright. Again, encouraging belief in the theory of evolution.

One hundred and fifty years was all it took to go from absolute God-fearing, Bible-believing people to... well, let's just say, I'm definitely worried about who we are now.

We have not only become a world of more anger and hate since schools removed the teaching of creation and embraced Darwinism, but society has also grown a pronounced hatred towards our Creator.

The only reasonable analogy for our existence is that this planet, with all of its intricately built complex processes, could only be of God. I have done enough research of this topic to be assured of this.

Darwin, of all persons, suspected that we had been created by God, despite his attempts to disprove the Bible. Other than a 'god' creator, there is no other logical explanation for our existence.

At the end of the day, God has given all of us the freedom to make our own decisions even though he would prefer that *everyone* believe and trust in him. We all have the ability to choose.

You might disagree with this choice. You may call God unfair, a tyrant, unloving, and mean spirited. But, it's pretty black and white. God made us, and he genuinely cares about us. We are *His* children.

What a magnificent place the Earth would be if we all stopped ignoring God and obeyed his rules (the Ten Commandments). There would be no crime, and there would be no fear. Only happiness and love.

Why would I be so naive as to believe that God doesn't exist. Furthermore, all we need to know is contained in God's book.

For example, how to care for the environment, how to respect nature, how to treat animals, and, most importantly, how to coexist with one another.

All this by chance you say— ***I think not.***

Chapter Five

Darwin's Playmates

"See to it that no one takes you captive by philosophy and empty deceit, according to human tradition, according to the elemental spirits of the world, and not according to Christ."
Colossians 2:8

I honestly would very much like to get into the word of God in the Bible, but I think it is important to first present the facts about what we have been led to believe over the past one hundred and fifty years.

To put it plainly… I am going to expose the lies.

We're going to get somewhat technical, but don't worry if you don't grasp everything. That isn't the most important factor. What is crucial is that you'll see that not all of the information with regard to the evolutionary theory has been shared with us.

Let's begin with an overview of the various types of science.

'Experimental Science' is not concerned with facts; rather, it is concerned with probabilities based on cause and effect. 'Empirical science' is another science that relies on observation and experience.

These two sciences form the basis of the evolutionary theory. What isn't acknowledged is that the conclusions from these sciences aren't 'facts' in the traditional sense.

Valid science must be trustworthy, have integrity, dependability, and reliability. Verification tools such as testing and measuring are also crucial, and because repeatability is another instrument used for validation, scientific research should be structured in such a way that testing methods can be replicated over and over, especially when published in scientific publications.

The definition of science has evolved over the past century and is still fiercely debated as to how it should be defined. But science isn't a point of view. It should be a neutral system that provides us with means to obtain and examine evidence on its own.

In order for something to be a fact, it has to be proven scientifically. To prove a theory scientifically, it must be observable and testable.

This is not possible with evolution. Everything we know, including the dating of artifacts, is nothing more than an educated guess— a probability (experimental science). This is a common misunderstanding.

I agree that these scientists have studied for many

years to produce these educated guesses, but the dominant problem stems from their viewpoint being very one-sided. When only one view of information is presented, it is never equal to a view from an unbiased opinion.

Evolution denies an intelligent creator, assuming that time, chance, and natural processes are the forces responsible for the material world and claims this alone.

The result of this is a philosophical, non-scientific concept that cannot be tested or verified. There are only assertions that these evolutions have occurred.

Evolutionary theories also shape beliefs that are not really open to debate. It has brainwashed society and, more dangerously, our children. This worries me because they will never be offered all of the facts or points of view in order to make an informed decision for themselves because evolutionists have identified their theory as the origin of life.

Evolutionists are free to express their views, and creationists are not, so we are being told what to believe because evolutionists have declared *their* theory as the cause of life.

When we are told something is probable numerous times, we tend to start to believe it.

Let's take a look at the 'ape to man' evidence for evolution. Quite often, we hear of transitional forms in evolution. These forms, that are just mere theories, are always taught as facts in our educational systems, as well as in the natural history museums throughout the country. But I believe there is another side to this story that is being left behind because evolution is an ever-changing story.

So, I spent a considerable amount of time digging up these so-called 'facts' from evolution science, and here is what I have found.

In 2005, after sequencing genomes, scientists declared that we share 98% of our DNA with chimps, thereby proclaiming them to be our closest relatives. Now, ninety-eight percent sounds pretty convincing. However, after digging a bit deeper, I also found many problems with this data.

Genomes are described as an organism's complete set of genetic instructions that are made up of DNA, but there is a problem with the scientists' analogy of the information because they have not fully disclosed *all* the information that they have found.

Not only that, they also did not use all the DNA available in the experiments to come to this conclusion. As a result, the lack of complete DNA information disclosure, coupled with only using a portion of it, shows a huge difference in outcome when compared to using all of the DNA.

For example, if scientists analyze the data using all of the available DNA, the 98% match they claim of humans sharing DNA with chimps drops to just 66–86%. This is a substantial change and shifts the entire evolutionary theory.

You must then surmise that maybe we are not as closely related to chimps as scientists portray us to be.

But wait, it gets better.

Chimps also have between 35 and 130 million more base genome pairs than humans, but in the studies, scientists have excluded 25% of the human genome material and 18% of the chimp genome material.

Why have they done that? Because without excluding this information, evolution does <u>not</u> work.

How then can you draw accurate conclusions from manipulated experimental data? Good question.

Scientists' predictions of millions and billions of years for their theory is simply not enough time for all those necessary natural mutations to have occurred.

In other words, scientifically speaking, evolution is not possible *without* the manipulation of information. This fact alone should start to send up red flags in your mind.

Here is yet another fact to ponder.

As science and technology becomes better and better, scientists have also realized that we actually share the same genetic code with many different animals and plants in the same 66–86% (truthful) range as chimps. There is nothing on earth that human beings share 98% of their DNA with. We share the same percentage of DNA with plants as we do with chimps.

It's funny that scientists don't seem to claim that we have also evolved from plants and other animals too, do they. I suppose that making the connection between human evolution and plants sounds silly and unrealistic. So, because chimps' overall structure is more like a human, it is an easier sell.

What exactly is DNA?

DNA is described as 'deoxyribonucleic acid' and is a molecule that contains the biological instructions that make each species unique. That incredible, tiny molecule that looks like a miniature winding staircase, passes down genes from generation to generation through the miracle of procreation; making babies. This is how we inherit the traits of our relatives. It is the chemical instructions for building our bodies and keeping us alive, but also, because of DNA, each one of us is different from one another. DNA is clearly miraculous.

It doesn't only make each one of us unique; if you unravelled all the DNA in your body, it would reach to the sun and back again multiple times.

When you really think about it, if we do not have the exact same, or close to the exact same DNA as chimps, how could we possibly have evolved from them?

But how then do we explain life?

A simple and sensible explanation would be that our incredible Creator has put a super complicated system in place for life. Life works the same way in humans as it does in every animal and plant, through DNA. It is the *essence* of life itself and it is in every living cell. How could a miraculous thing such as DNA have come to be without God? DNA is so complicated.

Is it plausible that it could have randomly evolved from chaos, or a single cell, or nothing at all? Nope.

Besides, there are obvious differences between humans and primates. We, as humans, believe in justice, truth, and righteousness. Chimps do not have that cognitive ability; they never have and never will. You cannot reason with a chimp.

Humans have developed laws and court systems in order for us to have a process in place to ensure rules and ethics are adhered to. Think of how society would manage without the structure of a legal system. That system allows us, the humans, to live on this earth without the world becoming a chaotic 'free for all'.

In society, if someone makes the choice to do wrong, we will chase that person halfway around the world to bring them to justice. Chimps don't do that. This is a very definitive difference between us (the humans) and chimps.

On the outside, we might slightly resemble primates, but in fact, we are very different.

But let's go back to the scientific comparison. In order for humans to seem more closely related to primates, scientists went as far as to change the chromosome data in chimps. Yeah, they did.

The human chromosomes differed from the chimps having 23 instead of 24, and they were unable to explain the difference. But to make the theory more plausible, scientists made the determination that human chromosome number 2 must have 'somehow' fused together over time with another chromosome. How else could scientists explain that there were 23 instead of 24 chromosomes? They couldn't. So, they once again manipulated the data by relabeling the chimp's chromosome number 2, to become 2A and 2B.

And just like that— the problem was solved. Chimps now had 23 chromosomes just like humans.

However, differences such as these are usually not reported to mainstream science because they mess up the evolution theory and timeline. The less explaining they have to do, the better.

There are also many problems with their so-called 'fusion site.' In reality, genomes are created with a cap to prevent this type of fusing. It's called a telomere.

In every living animal where there is a documented fusion or breakage located in chromosomes, there is also a specific type of sequence called 'satellite DNA'.

Within the scientist's explanation of the fusing of the chimp's chromosome 2, the fusion signature was missing the Sat DNA, and it was also only 798 bases letters long. It should have been between 10,000 and 30,000 bases long, not 798.

Again, absolutely no facts were presented by the

scientists. They managed to twist enough data to make the science work in favour of their projected outcome.

In reality, however, mutations do exactly what they are supposed to do— scientists just won't tell you about them.

So, why does so much of the information presented by evolution science have to be manipulated for it to work?

Well, because... if the scientists had not 'cherry picked' a portion of the data, their conclusions would have been very different, and the data would not have conformed to the scientists' explanation of evolution. It actually goes against what they claim.

Another trick up scientists' sleeve is using fossil evidence to back up their evolution story. But when you look closely at the evidence scientists use to describe a correlation between humans and chimps, it does not show any proof of this either. It simply doesn't add up and I'll show you why.

Here is what the scientific literature says about the most notorious primates in the evolutionist's timeline of transformation.

Let's begin with **"ARDI" (4.4–3.8 million years ago):** There are conflicting reports, but some reported information says that it took three years for scientists to dig up the remains of Ardi. Other papers have reported that it took fifteen years. OK, whatever...

but in total, 110-125 different specimens were found.

Now when I hear this, I think, "Wow, that's great. Specimens, that must mean actual full skeletal remains were found."

But no, it doesn't. It means archaeologists found 110–125 *pieces*, and not even intact bone pieces. Scientists found mostly bone fragments and many of them were described as being in 'terrible' condition. These remains were also found in a thirty-square-foot area and not all together as scientists would have you think.

Biologists called this example of an early hominid, "The most complete specimen ever found." They go into great detail about how Ardi 'likely' walked upright, what it ate, and when its social and reproductive changes occurred. Wow, it's like they were almost there to witness Ardi's life. And imagine all this with only analyzing bone fragments.

The skull bones of Ardi were so compressed that they had to be digitally reconstructed. Yes, digitally. Which also means the bones could have been reconstructed in any way they deemed suitable.

As well, archaeologists found zero bones from the base of the skull where the spine would have attached; meaning that in no way could they have determined with certainty that Ardi would have walked upright, even though this is what they absolutely imply.

This amazing 'early human', as they describe it, was up to 3'9" tall and weighed approximately 110 pounds; the same size as a chimp. Surprise, surprise.

To top it off when, looking at the 'questions' portion of a natural history museum website, Ardi's pelvic bone is described as being reconstructed from crushed fossils.

It is also stated that, "They don't know everything about the early ancestors, but they keep learning more!"

Some scientists argue that the evolutionary hypothesis cannot be verified because of a lack of credible evidence. Again, they 'hope' to answer questions with future discoveries. Like what Darwin had hoped.

In reality, not too many hard facts actually came from this discovery, just a lot of best guesses. Very scientific indeed! Not really...

Coming in at **(3.7-3.3 million years), we now have "LUCY":** Lucy is described as the 'leading specimen' for transitional change. She is plastered all over museums and textbooks in our educational system and has been reconstructed to walk upright, even though no actual hand or foot bones were ever found. Only a misidentified metatarsal (finger) bone that belonged to a human.

Lucy was a staggering 3'7" tall and weighed 64 lbs. Scientists describe her as having a small brain, and she was identical to a chimp in every way: a bonobo chimp. Except, they concluded that she might have had a different pelvis. Perhaps...

When it came time to reconstruct Lucy, the scientists had to reshape her pelvic bone with a grinder to fit the joint bones together.

Now 'reshaping' sounds very official, but I think I would consider that reshaping more along the lines of 'altering' the bone.

How can you presume anything from a supposed 3.5-million-year-old bone? It might have been crushed or part of it may have been missing. It's possible that it might not have even been from the same creature. This is an incredible amount of supposed time for something to be considered preserved and still intact enough to be assumed that it was as it would have been when it was still alive.

Scientists talk about these findings as if they knew for absolute certain how Lucy acted and what she ate. They really have no idea. Scientists are guessing based on today's primates. But that's OK, because she actually *was* one of them.

The museum of natural history displays Lucy as a life-like reconstructed model with all kinds of human features that cannot be proven. This includes things such as white eyes and arched feet, even though no foot bones have ever been found. This depiction makes her seem almost human without any factual evidence to support that conclusion.

What is not announced in their findings, however, is that they also found a lower femur and part of a shinbone (that they assumed was Lucy's) two and a half kilometres from where Lucy was found. These bones were also at least sixty meters deeper than Lucy's other bones.

Do you think there is a pretty good chance that

these bones didn't belong to Lucy?

But let's just assume these bones were Lucy's. If you include them with the other bones found, a total of four hundred specimens were found in the twenty-square-meter area that was sifted. And in those twenty tonnes of dirt, not one specimen of bone fragment was a complete bone, and, most of her skull was missing. Where is the evidence?

What archaeologists also don't tell you is that thirty percent of these bones were teeth. Yet we seem to believe this crazy story enough to use it as factual textbook material in our schools. Now, that *is* crazy.

Also discovered in this evolutionary time period was a series of footprints, but there were substantial problems with these as well. The footprints looked to have been made by modern humans, not hominids.

In an article on this subject from a story on a world history website, a British paleoanthropologist enlisted the help of a primate morphologist to determine the validity of footprints found in Laetoli.

It was discovered that the footprints, instead of showing a connection to Lucy, only confused the scientists more because they resembled a human's footprint.

The hope of the scientists was to connect these footprints to Lucy in order to strengthen their belief in the evolution of the bipedal, but because they showed an arched foot and no 'knuckle dragging' impressions, it was determined that these two to three sets of footprints belonged to something similar to a modern human.

Hmmm... it's interesting that scientists have evidence of human footprints in this time period, but feel they need to find some evidence to explain them away. This discovery also instigated a great debate in the scientific community that caused scientists to reconsider what they had previously thought about the human evolutionary theory.

Do you think there might perhaps be an issue with how scientists portray Lucy?

Much like Darwin, scientists are still hoping to find more fossils in the future so they can prove their theory. I really don't think this is the way it works in real life.

Then we get to **"HOMO HABILIS" (2.9–1.8 million years ago):** Besides a few skulls that were found with uncertain origins, the fossil record from this supposed age can fit into a shoebox... with enough room left over for a nice pair of shoes!

Homo Habilis has never been found in its entirety. But, in the museums of natural history, Homo Habilis is shown in its complete form even though there are hardly any transitional specimens dated to this time. Of the one hundred pieces found in a very large area, only a few skull fragments were found.

Also found in those one hundred pieces is a jaw with thirteen teeth, a molar, and twenty-one finger, wrist, and hand bones. However, later on, six of those bones were quietly confirmed as being from other animals.

This site also had other discoveries. Just below the surface were approximately twelve-foot round bases of hut foundations. Along with these foundations were stacks of heaped rocks that were two to two and a half feet apart and described as places to hold poles for grass huts. They also discovered more foundations buried beneath these ones, meaning the second discovery of foundations was even older than the first ones.

Outside of the huts, many bones of butchered animals were also found. Which totally makes sense. Of course, they butchered animals outside of the hut.

Of the many tools found, one type of stone tool was made of quartzite. It was very specific and would have had to have been quarried from many miles away. Also similar to the modern-day Nomadic people, they made choppers, scrapers, poly herons, discoids, burins, and flaked tools.

It sounds to me like they WERE, in fact, nomadic people.

In the next million or so years, scientists discovered **"HOMO ERECTUS".** This was called a 'transitional' period, and it was used to explain why Homo Erectus walked upright versus the movement of knuckle-dragging chimps. Again, with little or no proof of these creatures and plenty of artistry in their depictions, of course,

After that, **the "NEANDERTHALS" (350-300 thousand years ago):** Neanderthals were presented as 'primitive cavemen' using clubs and spears. But in fact, the Neanderthals had human DNA.

It is *thought* by scientists that Neanderthals gradually disappeared through interbreeding with humans. They believe small amounts of Neanderthal DNA may have been absorbed into the human race through this interbreeding.

If there were humans and they were alive at the same time, could Neanderthals possibly have been like some of today's remote tribes? That would make way more sense.

Neanderthals even had burial rituals because they actually buried their dead. Found in their burials was jewellery and things such as purses. Archeologists discovered that they also created music and art, and not surprisingly, they dove for seashells just as we do.

Theories about why Neanderthals went extinct continue to puzzle scientists who study human evolution.

Scientists say, "It was a very small group."

I suppose being a small group makes it more believable than if they were a non-human group that went extinct. They sound pretty human to me.

There are currently far more scientists attempting to explain evolution than there is physical evidence for it. With mostly bone fragments from only a few dozen skulls, the majority of the evidence for the whole five to seven-million-year human line can fit into the back of a pickup truck.

I honestly couldn't help but laugh to myself when I was researching this information. The theory is so ridiculous when your mind is not programmed to be in absolute awe of every new discovery and explanation. Even when I was a non-Christian, I never truly believed in evolution, but like most of you, I never really thought much about what we were being taught either. This research has definitely opened my eyes as well.

Think about what they have told us. Scientists claim that the universe and humans evolved from absolutely nothing.

OK, stop right here. For starters, this is impossible. We had to start somewhere because you can't make something out of nothing.

Let me ask you, "Do you believe that nothing creates everything?"

I'm certain your answer is no. Simple common sense tells us there had to have been something to begin with. This is also what most scientists believe.

However, a true atheist genuinely believes that everything was created from nothing. If you don't follow this line of thought, you are a theist, meaning you are not sure. Our problem is that we haven't thought about this information enough ourselves.

Here is a summary of the evolutionist's claims. Tell me if this seems plausible: From nothing, an incredible and perfect universe was created. And from that perfect universe, an incredible and perfect earth was created. And from that incredible and perfect earth, an incredible and perfect atmosphere was created. And from that perfect atmosphere, somehow bacteria formed and became a perfect single cell, which then formed into perfect seeds and plants. Then somehow, the cell also became algae, and then algae became a sponge-like creature that grew skin... which eventually evolved into a fish, which then grew four legs and walked on land.

Then, that fish-like land creature somehow lost all of its scales and grew hair in order to develop into an ape-like creature with a small brain. That ape-like creature eventually started to walk upright, and his arms eventually shrank, and his back straightened out, and his hands and feet changed, so he could use them to make things... and walk.

Then, the ape-like creatures 'dark chimp eyes' suddenly became 'white' like ours, and his pupils were now coloured. Wow.

Eventually, the ape-like creature lost almost all its hair, especially on the females. Oh yeah, now there are females! Because without females, they couldn't procreate.

So then, this ape-like creature became more human-like and somehow grew a bigger brain, so it was much smarter than our chimp ancestors. It (we) could now problem solve and we then miraculously learned to talk and communicate with words that we could understand — and in many different languages. Wow again.

And now, because we could figure things out, we also built tools so we could build shelters because those caves were kind of gloomy. These tools also helped us hunt and eat.

Unbelievably, we also suddenly discovered fire, so we could now cook our food however we wanted. When the food was medium rare, it tasted so much better.

We were now so civilized. And because we were now civilized, we decided it was a good idea to get married, have a family, and name our kids... and the dog.

Then, of course, educating our kids was the next reasonable step in evolution. We discovered that if we educated our kids, our offspring could now also have important careers and work many hours to have nice houses... and fast cars... and fancy boats... and go on expensive vacations and save money to send their kids to college. And then, we could save for retirement and... what?

Read this again so it really sinks in. I'm no scientist, but all this from nothing? And they say the Bible is hard to believe— what a joke!

You know, science used to be described as, "A quest for the truth and the study of evidence for that truth".

Science is now a 'priesthood', and if you don't follow the prescribed creed, you are then executed from your career. Unfortunately, the age of deceit is upon us.

I hope this was both educational and entertaining, but my job now is to show you how the Bible offers the answer to the 'how and why' we were created by God.

There is an incredible amount of science to back up the Bible, and in fact, there is way more evidence for the biblical creation account than there is for the evolutionary theory. The problem is, we are never told the entire truth.

However, I am going to tell you the truth, and I sincerely hope you continue reading this book to realize the importance of why we should...***trust the Bible and God.***

Chapter Six
The Big Book

---

*"Everyone then who hears these words
of mine and does them will be like a wise
man who built his house on the rock"*
Matthew 7:24

The Bible. What exactly is that big book with a lot of words? You know... the book we don't like to talk about and find difficult to understand. The same book we can't seem to make time for. Yes, that book.

Why do so many people shy away from reading the Bible?

Well, for starters, it is a book that some people feel may be controversial, and for others, it's difficult to read and understand. But the main reason for not reading the Bible is simple: It convicts us. Yes, the word of God convicts us of what we are doing wrong; and let's face it, we don't really want to hear about it.

After all, we are doing the best we can in this difficult world. Right?

And because we, as people, wholeheartedly resist the Bible and God, more and more doubt is then placed on our hearts, resulting in us intentionally blocking out God. This is our biggest issue as humans. We often choose not to hear God because we think our lives would suck if we followed him.

I used to think being a Christian meant you couldn't do anything fun. Not true. I am still the same person with the same interests, but God has definitely improved my life. To be honest, I feel now that I am not only true to myself, but also true to the truth and God. I finally have actual happiness.

Our God is an amazing God! He is so GOOD. Not like any goodness that we can comprehend. His goodness is unlike anything we have ever known here on earth.

That sounds kind of weird, I know. But think about it. If God made us, why would he not want to teach us and be with us? I'm sure you would also want to be with the kids you made and teach them. What's the difference? Just because God doesn't physically show himself to us doesn't mean that he doesn't love us deeply.

You also know, that as a parent (if you are a parent), you can't force your child into anything. Children must choose and make decisions when it comes to listening to a parent or they may receive punishment.

This is the same thing that God is telling us in the

Bible. Choose to listen or receive punishment. God wants us to make the right choice so very badly, and just the same as a parent who wouldn't want to see their child go down the wrong road, God doesn't want to lose any of us down the wrong road either.

When I ask people why they stopped reading the Bible, I often hear them say, "It just wasn't for me."

Wasn't for you? That's crazy. It is for every single one of us! This is what we fail to realize.

It is so difficult to describe what an amazing book the Bible is.

Many people will say the Bible is 'false until proven true.' But in fact, it is the only true word of God. I didn't always think that way, but now I fully believe that it is. No other religious book is written with nearly as much prophetic and historical accuracy as the Bible.

Books such as the Koran, Buddhist teachings, the Book of Mormon, as well as other religious bibles such as the Catholic bible, have all been adapted to man's ideas with their plans and words... not God's.

The facts in the true Bible (such as the English version KJV) have been checked and verified over and over throughout the millennia. You would think that non-Christian scholars and theologians would argue about the legitimacy and accuracy of the Bible, but they don't. It's legit.

The Bible is also the most sold book in the world, with over five billion copies sold and counting. That surely must mean something. If people were not curious about God, what would prompt billions of people to read the Bible? And if it was in fact a 'fake book', wouldn't you think people would have figured that out a long time ago?

Why are the ancient writings of the Old Testament also still around after thousands and thousands of years, and the New Testament after almost two thousand years?

Comparatively, the Koran (Quran) was written incrementally over a period of 23 years by one person (the prophet Mohamed) in the year 632. You cannot even begin to compare the incredible circumstances of the Bible's evolution to the Koran.

Another religious book, the Book of Mormon, had completed dictation in 1829 and went on sale for the first time in a bookstore in March of 1830.

This book was also written by one man, Joseph Smith, and it is reported that archaeological findings do not support the Book of Mormon, nor does it corollate with historical and paleontological evidence about the past, especially in the Americas. The evidence finds no parallel between the book and reported American archaeological sites.

As it turns out, the more analysis that is done on the Christian Bible, the more it becomes verified as true. The writings in the Bible have also withstood all the challenges from the many skeptics it has had. It is literally an *incredible* book.

So why do you suppose someone would desire to

read the Bible and continue to read it? It's not exactly a light read.

Well, for starters, I believe we all know there is a God Creator. God has given us a conscience written on our heart. 'Con-science' means 'with knowledge'.

The dictionary describes it like this: "an awareness of morality in regard to one's behavior; a sense of right and wrong that urges one to act morally."

Number two. Most of us desire to know if there is something more than just this life. Many of us feel that this life can't be all that there is. Humans have spirits and souls, and because of our souls, we feel a connection to the spiritual world.

And three, whenever you feel as if you should read the Bible, God is definitely working in you.

During our deepest times of despair, whether it is in faith or anger, if we ask God to show up— he will. I hope you choose to ask Him to show up. That's a great start because when you allow God into your life, the words in the Bible will come alive with understanding. Not only as to what those words mean, but you will also understand why God has said and done the things that he has.

The Bible is an amazing book that is written both literally and figuratively. Like I have said before, all the other religious writings, such as Hinduism, Buddhism, and Islam, started with a deity or 'god' and were re-written or added to by people. That addition of man's thoughts and words then persuades the direction of the reader to follow the religion's intention instead of God's intention.

I know what you're about to say, "How can you say that... people had to have written the bible too?"

You are correct. They absolutely did. The difference is the incredible conditions that had to come into play for the Bible to have been written and make sense. In no way could it have been possible without people being divinely inspired by God himself. The legitimacy of the Bible proves this, and the facts in the Bible tell the whole story.

Check this out. The Bible consists of sixty-six books that were written over a period of 1600 years by forty different authors. Not only that, it was also written on three different continents, in three different languages, and is comprised of over 780,000 words.

The authors typically did not know each other. It's not as if they could have called each other up and chatted about what to write to corroborate their stories. Yet, the Bible does not contradict itself throughout all of the 780,000 words.

These stories are not only fluid, they are also connected throughout the entire sixteen hundred years and have no errors other than a few translation errors. Typically, the translation error came from someone translating the text from one language to another. The total number of errors is less than one-fifth of one percent of the total number of pages in the book.

Let's break this down a little more. Sixteen hundred years is equivalent to approximately sixty generations.

In our average lifetime, we might experience three to four generations at the same time. Sixty generations are a very long time, especially for gathering information for a book.

Remember, these people did not have phones or computers back then. They didn't even have erasers. If the scribes made a mistake while replicating the words, the entire section was started over again to ensure the preservation of the original text.

The Bible is an entire library, with stories, murders, songs, poetry, and letters. It is not a fable, as some would perceive. In fact, it is actual recorded history that can be confirmed in many ways, such as with artifacts, art, the written word, and eyewitness accounts.

There are two main parts to the Bible. It starts with what is called the 'Old Testament.' This is the first book of the Bible. It describes the beginning of life, going back to the time of creation with Adam and Eve.

The Old Testament also records what happened at that time, and then it predicts what is going to happen in the future through prophecies.

The 'New Testament,' the second book, was written after Jesus died. It records that the prophecies in the Old Testament actually happened as foretold.

The prophecies from the Old Testament predicted such things as the birth, teaching and crucifixion of Jesus 'the Christ'.

The New Testament also predicts what is going to happen at what is called the 'end times.' The time that we are living in right now.

It is crazy to think that people wrote about what was going to take place in the future hundreds of years before it took place. But this is what happened, just the way God described that it would happen. There is absolutely no way the authors could have for-known the things that they wrote that many generations before they had happened. And if this was intended deception by the writers, wow, it was the best in history because the forty different authors' written works in this book fit together with engineered perfection.

Regardless of the doubters, the Bible is extremely accurate. I challenge everyone to read the entire book... then let's discuss it.

I know some of you will also say, "The words in the Bible must have been altered over the course of those years?"

No, they weren't as a matter of fact. And if you think they were, I also challenge you to look up the information yourself on how they were transcribed. You will be blown away by the meticulous care that was taken to ensure these words were not changed from the original text. This is yet another incredible attribute of the Bibles accuracy.

As doubters, why do we think this miraculous book was so difficult for God to create and why would we think that he doesn't know what's going on? If God created us (which I for one 100% believe that he did), then what would possess us to think that he couldn't create such an amazing book? A historical account of our world's creation and behaviour manual for the people in it.

Our problem is we tend to think in our 'human terms'.

Fair enough, as humans that's all we know. But we think we have life all figured out and that we can casually explain the Bible away. Yeah…that's wrong.

The Bible states that *anything* is possible with God— <u>not</u> with humans.

This is Gods promise to us. He has done so many things to prove his promises. Yet why do we continue to refuse to believe them? It is very easy to brush the Bible off as a book that compares to other religious books. I thought this too… until I read it. When you read it, the words in the Bible will hit you hard in your conscience.

I found myself wanting to skip many parts of it because it convicted me of what I was doing wrong. Like…seriously convicted me.

I was reading the words in the Bible and saying to myself, "Oh, that part wasn't really meant for me." I definitely wasn't ready to hear it— yet.

For example, I would read:

Luke 18:25 **"For it is easier for a camel to go**

through the eye of a needle than for a rich person to enter the kingdom of God."

I reasoned to myself that I wasn't, in fact, 'rich' and that I was fine. That this verse didn't apply to me. I mean... I was doing OK financially; I had a house and stuff, and a little money saved, but I certainly wasn't rich... like actual rich people.

It's funny because as I was thinking this back then, I knew I was kidding myself. I liked money, I liked things, and I wanted what other people had, and compared to most people in the world, I was very rich.

It wasn't until many years later, after feeling much closer to God, that I realized my attitude had changed. I no longer cared so much about stuff... or other people's stuff. My financial situation was even better than it was before, but it no longer mattered. This verse sums it up beautifully.

Matthew 5:3 "Blessed are the poor in spirit, for theirs is the kingdom of heaven."

Poor in spirit, it was exactly that. I realized that God wanted me to put him first. I didn't have to sell everything and become homeless. The need to want more and more was no longer in my thoughts, or the desire to want what others have. I just wanted God and I trusted that he would look after me. The *best* day of my life for sure!

The Bible was truly given to us as our instruction

book for life, but so many of us don't like the words of the Bible.

I agree, they are difficult words to hear. They are hard words to hear because they convict us of all the stuff we do wrong, especially in the sight of the God who created us.

Just think about it. If you had robbed a bank yesterday, the last thing you would want to do is have dinner tonight with a policeman. You *know* that he would likely sense your guilt.

Most of us feel the same way about God. We don't want anything to do with God because we know we are guilty of the things we have done wrong. It's easier to ignore God than face him, even though our conscience tells us those things were wrong and we shouldn't have behaved like that.

Think about the Ten Commandments. How many of those commandments have we broken over and over? I truly think this is why people choose different types of religions. Humanity will try to find the one religion that makes them happy and won't convict them of what the Bible teaches.

"So what?" you say, "What is wrong with believing in other religions?"

Many people think that if you believe in 'something' that is the most important thing, even if it isn't the Christian Bible. I mean, as long as your religion brings you happiness and we treat people decently, we are doing good for God, right?

Well... no, actually.

This is my point. I'm not trying to deter you from being kind to your fellow man or woman. We should all do our best to help our fellow humans. But you absolutely cannot bribe God in order to get a ticket to heaven and have everlasting life with him. God gives the ticket to you freely.

I'll explain.

Almost every religion promises an afterlife in one way or another when you die. However, Christianity is different. It doesn't require you to do 'good works' or pray at certain times of the day to earn the right to an afterlife.

For example, Hinduism, teaches that 'what you will return as' in the afterlife, is dependent on your behaviour here on Earth. Hinduism says that you could possibly come back as a rat or some other animal if you were a bad person; all the way up to returning as a prince if you were a good person. That's a HUGE range. And who decides this?

Buddhism, on the other hand, denies that God even exists. It refers to life as an illusion of sorts. Buddhism might make you feel good and ease your fears for a time, but it too will not help you when you die.

Islam acknowledges that there is sin and hell. But it is also a works-based religion, offering you escape from hell if you do good works. If you are a follower of Islam and are sincere in your repentance at the time of your death, you are promised to go to the afterlife, similar to other religions, such as Mormonism… but for this, you had better correctly guessed your time of dying.

The problem is that if you truly believe in a Creator God, you are wasting your time belonging to any other religion than Christianity. Especially if those religions don't believe the words written in the Bible or if those religions don't follow those words seriously.

It is like contributing to a 'cause' you believe in and then finding out it's a fraud. You've wasted a lot of time and money.

Believe me. God knows we are ***all*** messed up. None of us, according to his definition, are good, and we cannot possibly do enough 'good things' to make up for our mistakes. We all believe that if we are decent, hard-working people, we will go to Heaven. This belief is incorrect and probably the most important and difficult one for us to grasp… because again, we are using our human philosophy to determine our destination.

Mark 10:18 And Jesus said unto him, "Why callest thou me good? there is none good but one, that is, God"

This is why Jesus is so important. God sent his only Son (Jesus) to take away the burden of our sins stemming from our sinful behaviour. In exchange, God ONLY asks that we repent (change our ways) and trust in His son, Jesus Christ. God gives us this gift freely, and it is our choice to accept it... or not.

We are in full control; this is the way humanity likes it to be.

Just think for a moment. What would this world be like if all of us in the world were to follow the commandments that God gave us? Would it be different than what we are experiencing today? God gave us ten simple commandments. How hard could it be to follow them?

Let's see if I can explain the Ten Commandments in terms that are a bit easier to understand.

#1 <u>You shall have no other gods before me</u>

OK, so what does this mean? Honestly, I didn't know either, but after reading the Bible and looking at what we consider 'gods' in this world, I get it now.

In our human terms, we think of 'gods' as what was described back in the days of ancient Egypt. The people of that day worshipped golden statues of goats, pigs, and cows. From these different types of idols, they also made different styles of religion.

Today, however, it's not only about worshipping different icons of religion, but it is also about us idolizing famous people or groups. We seem to have zero time for God and set aside our Creator to ignore him because we would rather focus our attention on someone or something else.

This is what God means by saying, "Have no other 'gods' before Him."

Compare this instruction to that of a parent who has a child that is not obeying them. As a parent, you would say to your child, "You must listen to me, as I am your parent. I love you and know what's best for you." But the child, in their ignorance, wants to take control of their actions. You cannot, as a loving parent, allow your child to make decisions without your guidance because this would be harmful to them.

Well, that is what God is saying to us. He truly loves us and doesn't want harm to come to us either. So, God wants us to act as he has instructed us to act. God is no fool. Not only does He *see* the big picture… HE *is* the big picture.

On the contrary, we humans, unfortunately, cannot see what is actually happening most of the time because we are arrogant. As a result of that pride, we stray further and further from God's rules, ending up having no idea of what being close to God is all about. So then, in turn, we make 'imaginary' gods disguised as Spiritualism to suit our unrepentant hearts.

Just look at what is going on in the world. It's shocking. We are falling apart at the seams. Why is this happening?

Another example of a 'god' we worship is... you guessed it, money.

Of course, we all love money and can't live without it. However, when you love money *more* than you love God, the money then becomes a type of 'god'. It becomes all that we can think about, and all we want is MORE of it.

I'm not saying to you that you can't have money, but if money, or anything else for that matter, becomes the most important priority in our lives, then that *is* a problem.

Don't get me wrong, I totally get this and am guilty of this too. It's hard not to fall into the 'stuff trap' because we are constantly surrounded by so many things that can stimulate our desire to believe that we absolutely need these things. I have definitely struggled with this many, many times.

And yes, you are right again, it is in our human nature to 'want'. How is it possible to ever be free of 'want' without God?

One other thing that has become a modern false god is social media. Far too often, I too find myself getting sucked into the social media vortex when I have purposely sat down to spend time with God. By the time I finally look up from my device, two hours have passed by, and I no longer have time for God. I put social media pleasure ahead of God's pleasure. Totally unacceptable.

I think if it was me who created all these people and they were unthankful and chose to ignore me, I'd be upset too! <u>In simple terms</u>: **Put God first**

#2 <u>You shall not make for yourself a carved (or graven) image</u>

Umm... what? We don't really consider a 'carved

image' to be something we have readily on hand in today's age, do we?

Ahhh... but maybe we do?

Essentially, this commandment speaks about things we might idolize. Things that we don't even realize.

This might sound hypocritical coming from someone who believes in God but think about 'religious' items.

What about statues of the Saints or the Virgin Mary? Christians don't worship these things... religious people do. God asks us to not put anything before him.

Also, think about religious leaders who believe themselves to be 'spiritually higher' than everyone else. They, too, become an image of worship within their religion. Even if the religious leader started with the best of intentions, as humans, they begin to love the 'fame and fortune' that comes with being a type of celebrity. This leads to real conflict within the word of God. The same word of God message that they are trying to convey in their religion. These people become false idols, taking credit for God's goodness.

What about symbols in our world? We wear them, we see them, and we praise them. For example, we might have trinkets that we have collected from travels around the world, such as stones, carved artwork, or perhaps a religious carving.

There's nothing at all wrong with having these

things, but if they become something that we choose to worship spiritually, then that is a problem.

We also have many things in our society that represent symbols or symbolism. Don't worship these things. Just worship God. <u>In simple terms:</u> **Don't worship other things**

#3 <u>You shall not take the name of the Lord your God in vain</u>

OK, this is a big one and we don't even realize this because we have all sworn (cussed) before. We can't seem to help it when things don't go our way. The words come out of our mouth without even thinking about it.

I love watching Ray, the street preacher, who does interviews. He speaks to ordinary people, asking them their views on God and the afterlife. In all his videos, he asks the same question, "Have you ever sworn?"

Of course, we have. How many times have we used the words 'Godd#@n' or 'JesusC&!$t' as a swear word when we are upset or angry? We even say 'OMG' when we are shocked or disgusted with something.

However, if you are using this phrase in the context of swearing, you are blaspheming God. Yep... maybe just a figure of speech, but why God's name and not anyone else's?

Umm, well... *everyone* says it. So, no big deal... right?

The fact is, we have been conditioned to speak this way. Are we perhaps rebelling like a teenager would against authority?

Here's the real question: Why do we think it's no big deal? Why do we use the names of our Creator and his Son in place of swear words to express our disgust?

Would you use your mother's name as a swear word? Of course, you wouldn't. She gave birth to you and raised you. Using her name to swear would totally dishonour her. Why, then, do we dishonour the name of our loving Creator and use it as a description of disgust or anger? Good question.

Did you also know this use of God's name was punishable by death in the Old Testament? Here is what God promises in the future at His return.

Matthew 12:36-37 "But I tell you that for every careless word that people speak, they will give an account of it on the day of judgment. For by your words you will be justified, and by your words you will be condemned."

Consider all of the historically evil people whose names we could have used to cuss. It would only make sense to use a hated person's name, but, have you ever heard someone use a phrase such as 'Hitler-d#@n or 'TedBundy&!$%'? Nope, we never have.

Why do you suppose this is? It's kind of crazy when you think about it. But I guess we *are* using a person we 'hate' to express disgust, because we obviously don't like God... or Jesus, if we speak about them in this way.

In reality, until the offence is pointed out, most of us don't even realize we are doing this. This is a very serious sin against God. Think about that before you let it slip out again. Break the habit, change your ways and ask for forgiveness and repentance. God is very gracious and forgiving. <u>In simple terms:</u> **Don't use God's name or the name of His Son Jesus to express disgust**

#4 <u>Remember the Sabbath Day, to keep it Holy</u>

Nope, this is not possible for most of us. Life is simply far too busy and far too complicated. Is God really asking me to use one of my two days off to do nothing but go to church and worship him? No way, I have so many things to do, and I also have a spouse who does not see the importance of this commitment.

This is one that I struggled with as the organizer of my family. To the fault of my own, I always seemed to find an excuse to justify why I couldn't go to church. There was always a project that someone needed a hand with, or maybe we had plans to go somewhere that day. I put God second… or even third, or fourth.

God wants us to make the time to read his word, pray and talk with him. He wants us to take a day off from this busy world in order for us to have a relationship with Him. That's why God asks us to set aside at least one day a week.

Honestly, though, we really should be making time for Him every day, not only when it is convenient for us. However, the closer you become to God, the more you will want to spend time with him. And when you start to make the time, you will clearly understand why it is so important to put Him first. <u>In simple terms:</u> **Make the time to worship God and read the Bible daily.**

#5 <u>Honor your father and mother</u>

Most of us love our parents and appreciate the wisdom that comes from them. Usually, it is not until much later in life that we can fully comprehend the role models our parents were throughout our childhood, and even though at the time we didn't care for the discipline we received in our childhood, we can certainly appreciate it as adults.

However, some of us have real issues with our parents. We can't choose our parents, and they too are real people dealing with real-life issues. Sometimes these struggles have deeply affected us as their children, and maybe, that impact has made it more difficult for us to honour them at all.

But then, as adult children having children of our own, it also becomes more evident as to how difficult life can be. Our parents are not perfect people… just like us.

Nonetheless, they may have done or said things that we find embarrassing or hurtful. Maybe their actions were just downright inconsiderate. How can you possibly respect and honour parents under conditions such as these? It becomes very difficult.

Despite this, I believe that the respect God is

referring to for us as children is to maintain dignity towards them, even though, in our own opinion, some parents might not deserve this dignity.

God is not asking us to pass judgement on anyone, especially our parents. So do not lie to them, swear at them, yell at them, or talk bad about them.

The bottom line is that they are our parents and they have given us life, without them... no us. They may not be perfect, and you may totally disagree with them, but they do deserve to be honoured respectfully. It does not have to have strings attached, simply don't be derogatory towards them. None of us are perfect. In simple terms: **Be respectful of your parents**

#6 You shall not murder

Well, this should be easy! Most of us have no desire to hurt or kill people. But what else does this mean?

Have you ever been so angry with someone and hated them so much that you could not forgive them? That deep hate consumes us. Then, as a result, it manipulates our lives. God considers this feeling of hate comparable to murdering someone.

So... does that mean that I can never be angry with someone?

Well, that's not reality. Life is hard. People do so many stupid things that some of us find very difficult to tolerate. I think what we have to be aware of, is that level of frustration that can build to a boiling point, and when it does, frustration can come out as hatred.

Hate is one of those feelings that makes the hair on the back of your head stand up. It affects not only the health of our bodies but is also not great for our mental well-being.

God knows this, and what he doesn't want for us is to get to that stage of anger where we feel such hatred. Yet, as difficult as this may seem, God also wants us to pray for those who offend us.

Pray for them? You're kidding, right? I say, "No way, I'm not doing that."

But just a minute. Perhaps we should turn the table for a moment. I'm sure at some point in our lives we have all been that person who was hated for something we had said or done. We all mess up and hurt others. What would it be like to be on the receiving end of someone else's hate? Most of us know this feeling. It's not very pleasant.

I know it sounds difficult, but God wants us to be kind to those that hurt us or hate us. When we hate, God knows in our hearts that we despise those people to the point of not caring if they are dead or alive. So, tell me, what is the difference between that much hate and murder? According to God, not much. That is why He says this. <u>In simple terms:</u> **Do not murder, hurt, or hate**

#7 <u>You shall not commit adultery</u>

This is a difficult one for sure! Sex is the one thing that is on everyone's mind. It always has been.

So, what does this commandment mean exactly?

If I'm not married, will this apply to me? Or, if I have been faithful to my spouse, am I all good?

Well, not so fast...

Some religions will teach that sex is dirty. Not true. Sex is amazing, not dirty. God gave us this incredible intimate connection to feel pleasure and closeness with each other. But when you cross the line and have those intimate encounters with someone other than your spouse, the problem ignites.

The Bible also says that anyone who looks with lust commits adultery in their heart. What does this mean? All of us are human, and we can't help but look at people that we are attracted to.

This isn't the problem. When we fail is when those 'looks' lead to more, even if those thoughts only remain in the privacy of our mind. At that point, we have crossed the line.

It's amazing, as humans, how we instinctually have that feeling of 'cheating'. Yes, even if it is just a fantasy in our mind, some of us will feel like we have cheated.

Why do you suppose we feel this way, even though we have not physically cheated?

Sex was not given to people by God to use loosely or for us to feel good whenever we choose. Just because it is accepted by society to sleep with whomever we please, doesn't mean that it was God's intention for us to behave like this.

What great instruction this verse is! Too bad we have decided not to listen to it.

Jesus said in:

Matthew 19:3-5 The Pharisees also came to Him, testing Him, and saying to Him, "Is it lawful for a man to divorce his wife for just any reason?" He answered, "Have you not read that he who created them from the beginning made them male and female," and said, "For this reason a man shall leave his father and mother and be joined to his wife, and the two shall become one flesh? So they are no longer two, but one flesh. Therefore what God has joined together, let no one separate."

So, what about porn?

Again, porn is accepted as normal in today's society. Most everyone in the world today has either viewed video porn or has been exposed to it in one form or another.

Porn is a huge money maker, but the incredibly sad part about it is that it victimizes women, men, and, unforgivably, children as well. With every moment that passes, there are more and more children who are victimized by porn.

What is porn actually doing to us? Studies have shown that porn desensitizes us to the point that we can no longer have a normal, healthy sexual relationship. It is also super addictive. Only after a short time of viewing porn, a normal intimate relationship will never meet the expectations of the fantasy world seen online. As a result, porn becomes an extremely difficult to break addiction that causes a great deal of pain in life.

According to God, it was his intention for us to marry a spouse and fully enjoy sex with them... but with them alone, not with whoever we please. God does not want us sleeping around and having sex outside of marriage.

To some, this might seem impossible. They would ask, "What do you mean, I can only have sex with one person?"

Yes, this is, in fact, what the Bible states.

Here's the good news though... it's not impossible. For those who already have this relationship with their spouse, there is nothing better than this. Being able to have that deep love and trust with your spouse is a truly amazing feeling. The sense of being 'as one' rings true in this type of relationship. It is absolutely possible.

On the contrary, in a relationship where cheating begins... so does the secrecy. When secrecy begins, next comes distrust, and distrust is usually the start of a relationship breaking down. When relationships breakdown, the fighting begins, and then eventual separation. You know where it goes from there.

However, relationships are just too valuable to not make every effort to repair them, and God is both loving and forgiving, so don't think it's too late for you. In simple terms: **Do not cheat or look with lust**

#8 <u>You shall not steal</u>

This is crazy. Who hasn't? I am guilty of this for sure, as I can imagine most of you are.

What exactly drives our will to steal? And why from such an early age? It seems that as soon as we feel the need for the stuff we can't have, we have the urge to steal it. We want it, so we steal it. Simple.

Sometimes we use the 'Robin Hood' approach when we steal something that doesn't belong to us. We think we are stealing it for the 'greater good'.

For example, perhaps you know someone with a large pile of firewood, and instead of approaching the owner and asking for some, you go ahead and steal it... because it's just easier that way.

Ahh... but the wood is not for you. It is for the poor elderly person down the street who can't keep themselves warm. You justify your actions and don't feel guilty about them because it seems to be a 'just' cause.

Don't kid yourself, it's stealing. In this world, we twist our evil deeds around in our minds until we deem them justifiable. We like to make our own rules instead of obeying Gods.

How about stealing little things? Things of little or no value? As a child, I used to think it was OK to take fifty cents out of my mom's change container to go to the candy store. It was only fifty cents, and she would never know the difference in that huge container of change.

However, knowing what I know now, stealing

those fifty cents was no different than stealing fifty thousand dollars. It wasn't mine, but I took it anyway. I definitely stole it.

Here is another example. How many of us have downloaded music off the internet that isn't ours? Same thing. We don't consider it stealing because everyone does it. It seems trivial, yet it doesn't make it any less dishonest.

Another type of stealing is not being 'fully truthful.' I have been not fully truthful so many times I can't even count them all. I am ashamed to say it didn't bother me at all to lie in this way.

Think about it, though. Have you ever considered the cashier who accidentally forgot to charge you for the item in your shopping cart? You put that item in your cart, so obviously you wanted it and were willing to pay for it. Instead of being honest and making them aware of it, you felt like you had a bonus that day, like getting a '2 for 1' deal.

But did you perhaps consider that this cashier had to account for that item at the end of the day? Did you make the effort to go back and pay for it? Nope. Me neither. Guilty of lying and stealing... again.

How many 'shysters' are out there in this world cheating and robbing innocent people? We can't believe that *those* kinds of people would do such a thing to such good people. But what we fail to see is that even the smallest theft hurts someone, such as me not being fully truthful. Why do we think we are such fantastic humans that we deserve the things we haven't earned or paid for?

I am not arguing that stealing isn't in our human nature. Who hasn't stolen? We have all stolen in our lifetime; it's so difficult to change our ways.

However (I'm going to sound religious here), once I started to know and love God, my conscience became very black and white. There is no grey area anymore. You all of a sudden know exactly what to do, and I can't tell you how amazing that feeling truly is. In simple terms: **Don't take anything that doesn't belong to you**

#9 You shall not bear false witness against your neighbour

This is not meant literally for only your 'neighbor.' So, who is your neighbor then? Good question. The short answer is… everyone is our neighbour. God wants us to treat every single person with compassion and dignity.

What kind of description is 'bear false witness'? Are we in court? No… not yet anyway. This wording describes lying, plain and simple. There are many types of ways to bear false witness. We occasionally lie to protect people from hurt feelings that would otherwise result from being truthful.

We also use lies to make ourselves seem important. There are times when we don't tell the 'whole truth' because we fear it might damage our reputation, or we lie about ourselves to gain an edge over someone else in life.

Yes, I am guilty of this too.

Some of us lie to get ahead in our careers and financial situations, to cheat on spouses, or talk behind people's backs. We can also verbalize lies to people in order to express how we feel, all the while thinking something very different in our minds.

Unarguably, it is in our human nature to lie, and it is also a human trait that we adopt from a very early age. I guarantee, you will not find one person who hasn't lied— or they are lying if they tell you that they haven't.

Think of how we feel when we catch someone who has lied to us. I know I feel disappointed and hurt by that person. I think to myself, how could they not have told me the truth? It is almost a feeling of despair when you are faced with being lied to.

However, the worst feeling I've had, is when I have been caught lying to someone else. I feel humiliation, fear, guilt, and sorrow.

So why do we lie, knowing the outcome will be hurtful? I certainly don't have all the answers, but I know that I have lied to make myself seem like a better person to others, and when I ponder the fact that I actually lied to achieve a better person status, that lie has obviously proved my belief of me being a better person wrong.

This is such a difficult topic to give a simple answer to. Life is so very complicated. But what I do know is that lying almost always causes more hurt, trouble, and dissension than telling the truth. One small lie usually turns into many larger lies. God knows this too. Be true to yourself and God; be honest. <u>In simple terms:</u> **Tell the truth, always**

#10 <u>You shall not covet</u>

Covet? What does that word mean? In today's terms, we would say, "Don't desire all the stuff everyone else has."

I think for most of us, it is so hard to be happy with what we have because we are always aware of others with so much more than us. Other people always have the cool new stuff, and so, we think that life must be easier for them because they have the money to buy all these things.

How many of us wish we could have their house, or their car, or their furniture? We believe that we would be so much happier with better things.

What about their spouse or family? We think he/she is being treated so much better than I am, I would love to have their relationship instead of my dysfunctional one. Here's news for you… we all have dysfunctional relationships to some extent.

What about lifestyles? Why do I have to work so hard to get ahead when others seem to always have more than me?

Or better yet… how come they are so 'lucky' to win the lottery and I never win anything? Other people are so fortunate, and I'm not... it's just not fair.

Here's the thing in today's world: Most of us have put money and stuff way ahead of God, and that stuff makes us totally forget about him. We are constantly bombarded in this life with the importance of wealth and the perceived happiness that comes with it... status.

It consumes us to the point where, when we speak, we often feel it's necessary to include a form of 'status' in our conversations with others to elevate us, or whoever we are speaking about. Maybe it's our spouse or our children that we are being prideful about. Do you really feel that this is important?

Have you perhaps considered that the person you are talking with might not be as fortunate as you with their family or wealth? How do you think your boasting makes them feel? Has your pride helped *them* feel better about themselves... or only you?

I know, as humans, we all want to elevate ourselves in life to feel good, but it actually only helps us, not anyone else.

How do I know this? Yes... guilty. As difficult as it is, do your best to be humble.

I remember being in my twenties, working hard and finally being able to buy a bit more expensive stuff, and saying to myself, "Yep, whoever has the most toys in the end... wins."

How crazy was my attitude? It wasn't until I became much older that I realized... who really cares, and you care even less after you have had to deal with tragedy in your life. None of the 'stuff' matters anymore when you suddenly realize what is genuinely important.

Do you remember when 9/11 happened? We all feared we were going to be attacked, or that it may be the beginnings of a war. I remember seeing all of the famous, wealthy celebrities on TV claiming that after the twin tower tragedy, the only thing that mattered to them was their loved ones. When they were afraid for their lives, they admitted that money meant nothing to them.

Unfortunately, that feeling was temporary.

As humans formed by God, we are meant to care about people. Why do we need tragedies to realize that this is the *most* important thing in life? Why have we let wealth and stature overcome our concern for our fellow humans? As much as we'd like to think we do not do this, we judge others based on how their status compares to ours.

The Bible says we cannot love money and God. I understand this now, and just because I understand it, that doesn't mean I don't struggle with it. I think we all like nice things, and being human, we want those things no matter what the cost.

I hear you thinking. Yes, of course, money is required to survive. Money also gives us a certain amount of assurance in life. The assurance that we can buy the things we need to live comfortably. But when greed and coveting take over, that is where the problem lies.

We have an insatiable desire for more, and seeing our neighbors with more causes us to want what they have as well. Our 'god' becomes that desire. We then work harder in order to acquire more things, which makes us feel as if we have social status, and therefore we feel accomplished in this life. Why is it that we place such a high value on our social standing? Why is it that we regard status as such an important thing in life?

The problem with this ideology, is that it totally disregards the teachings of God. God doesn't tell us to have stuff and be happy… people do.

However, this is how humanity thinks because we are distant from God. We are not always happier when we have more. God created us, and only *He* understands what true happiness is. <u>In simple terms:</u> **Be happy with what you have, and also be happy for others.**

These 10 commandments of God make so much sense, that they actually are common sense. I challenge you to apply these commandments to the world today. What difference do you think these simple rules would make in the behaviour of mankind?

Just contemplate this idea for a moment. How much more peaceful and wonderful do you think the world would be if we followed the Ten Commandments?

Think about people's marriages. Without lying,

committing adultery, hating, and swearing, how would this change impact most of our relationships?

Obviously, the transformation would be HUGE, and the daily stress of relationships would all but vanish. Best of all, the effect of this shift would also trickle down to the children of that relationship.

Another positive effect of a Ten Commandments world would be seen in the lives of our kids. We wouldn't have to worry about our kids like we do today. Children would be able to play outside without the fear of someone hurting them or taking them. Kids could read any book or magazine... or watch any TV show. Parents wouldn't have to protect them from the internet or from other adult situations.

Children also wouldn't have to be witnesses to parents arguing or physically fighting. Families would have peaceful homes with both mom and dad living in love with each other and also in love with God.

A world where it would be OK to leave your wallet or phone somewhere by accident without fear of it being quickly stolen and you wouldn't have to worry about being scammed when buying something.

You could leave your house unlocked, your car unlocked, your bike unlocked. How awesome would that be!

Do you maybe think following the Ten Commandments could affect our work and social lives?

Without lying, stealing, coveting, hate, and lust, we would have solid friendships based on honesty and trust.

Yes, you are right, this *is* something we should already have, but it is also very challenging in today's world. It has become more and more difficult to be true friends with people because of differences of opinion and the rapid onset of cancel culture. We no longer have the ability to discuss topics as grown adults, especially if you are outside of the general ideology of the modern world view. The bottom line is that we can no longer be open and honest about who we are and how we think for fear of offending others.

I truly wish that we would care more deeply for every single person. When did we lose this part of humanity? People act as if they care, but they really don't. I also wish all people were treated the same, no matter their status, income, or race. Simply be kind and speak kindly to one another. We could share all that we have and help each other, care for elderly parents, care for the sick, and care for the lost and lonely. We seem to care too much about ourselves.

Instead, it seems to be survival of the fittest at its best. I am not saying that kind care doesn't happen at all today, but most of us are far too busy keeping up with life to find enough time to help other people.

Just imagine if everyone in the whole world had enough of everything and our purpose in life was to care for each other and be kind. A world that far exceeds this one in goodness, where there is never any pain, sadness, swearing, deceit, cheating, stealing, coveting, murder, or death. Can you picture an amazing world such as this?

Well, my friends, this wonderful place is called Heaven. God fully intended for this world to be that very place until evil took Adam and Eve over.

The good news is that God promises that perfect world to return soon. Adam and Eve, through 'personal choice,' screwed it up for us the first time.

If you read back to the first book of the Bible, in Genesis, God created an amazing world with enough food, plants, water, and animals. Everything we would need for a great life.

But God had a simple rule for the humans that he himself created in his own image. His instructions were straightforward.

Genesis 2:16-17 The LORD God commanded the man, saying, "From any tree of the garden you may freely eat; but of the tree of the knowledge of good and evil you shall not eat, for in the day that you eat of it you shall surely die."

It's not like this was the *only* tree in the garden that Adam and Eve had to eat from. There were many trees in the garden. But Adam and Eve were tempted by evil... much the same as all of us still are to this day.

This is <u>why</u> God sent us His son. *Jesus is up next...*

Chapter Seven
Why Jesus?

*The doctrines of Jesus are simple, and
tend to all the happiness of man.*
— Thomas Jefferson, third President

Who was Jesus? We hear the name Jesus all the time. But who really was this historical figure that has impacted all of our lives?

Whether we believe this or not, Jesus was a 'one of a kind' man; a prophet like no one else before him or after him.

Historians don't argue the fact that He was a real person, although some unbelievers try to tell us otherwise. So why is Jesus so important, and why have we tried to all but forget about him? What did Jesus do to us that was so awful to make us dislike him so much?

Jesus was the long-awaited 'Messiah' prophesied

in the Old Testament and referred to as God's Holy One. The Hebrews of that time were looking for a saviour, but their image of who that saviour would be, differed greatly from what the scriptures foretold. The Jewish people thought they were waiting for a flashy king— a great and powerful leader who was to save them. Not a poor carpenter.

Mark 6:3 "Is not this the carpenter, the son of Mary, and brother of James, and Joses, and of Juda, and Simon? And are not his sisters here with us?" And they took offense at him.

The most incredible part of Jesus' miraculous conception is the detailed plan of His birth, written long ago by the prophet Isaiah. More than 600 years before the birth of Jesus, the Christ.

Isaiah 7:14 "Therefore the Lord himself shall give you a sign; Behold, a virgin shall conceive, and bear a son, and shall call his name Immanuel."

The following is the history of Jesus' birth.

Jesus' mother, Mary, was a woman of great faith and purity who was engaged to be married. During the time of her engagement, the angel Gabriel appeared to Mary and told her of God's plan for her.

She was astonished by this visit and couldn't comprehend how she would become pregnant with a child since she was still a virgin, but she also had complete trust in God.

Luke 1:38 And Mary said, "Behold, I am the servant of the Lord; let it be to me according to your word." And the angel departed from her.

Mary's intended husband, Joseph, was a carpenter. Joseph deeply loved Mary, but they had not yet slept together when Mary told Joseph that she was pregnant.

When Joseph heard the news of her pregnancy, he knew the child was not his. Yet he did not want to bring shame to Mary, so he thought to himself of how he could quietly separate from her in order to not dishonour her. But then, the angel Gabriel came to Joseph in a dream and told him of God's plan as well. Joseph, being a man of faith, also believed Gabriel, and then took Mary as his wife.

This was undoubtedly an unusual situation at the time. When you were betrothed (engaged), you didn't sleep with your mate until you were married, but it wasn't as if no one had ever cheated on each other. Adultery did occur, but it was extremely unusual because if you were caught, you were almost certainly stoned to death.

The mere fact that Joseph stayed with Mary and chose not to separate himself from her is incredible.

For the most part, Jesus grew up as a normal Hebrew child being raised by his mother and father. Jesus also had many younger siblings who at first did not believe that he was anyone else other than their brother. But as they watched Jesus during the time that he became a public figure and then his subsequent crucifixion, they began to believe that Jesus possibly was the Messiah that was foretold to come from God.

As a matter of fact, two of Jesus' brothers later wrote letters that made up part of the New Testament in the Bible.

Not only did Jesus die, but he also resurrected from the dead. His body has never been reported. What exactly does it mean to 'rise from death,' and why is it significant?

Actually, this is everything.

To put it another way, Jesus not only foretold his own death, but also his resurrection from the dead, demonstrating that HE *is* God in the flesh. This Resurrection was Jesus' most amazing promise to us. We would not be able to depend on any of his other promises, such as conquering death, had He not risen from the dead. Not only conquering death for himself, but for believers in him as well.

John 7:33-34 **Jesus then said, "I am with you for a little longer, and then I am going to him who sent me. You will look for me and will not find me. Where I am you cannot come."**

Numerous eyewitness reports from Jesus' followers point to the fact that he appeared to them several times after they confirmed that he had been crucified on a cross.

Many times, Jesus told his disciples that he would be risen from death, but they didn't understand what that meant until after he died and then appeared to them in person. The witnesses who saw him claim that Jesus was not like a ghost. They said that He was, in fact, a real person who even showed them his wounds from the crucifixion. This is important.

Thomas (one of the twelve disciples) was not present the first time Jesus appeared to his disciples following his resurrection. If you've heard the phrase "doubting Thomas," you're probably unaware that it originates from this moment.

John 20:24 "Now Thomas, one of the Twelve, called the Twin, was not with them when Jesus came."

John 20:25 So the other disciples told him, "We have seen the Lord." But he said to them, "Unless I see in his hands the mark of the nails, and place my finger into the mark of the nails, and place my hand into his side, I will never believe."

When Thomas was told by the other disciples that Jesus had appeared to them, he refused to believe the story until he was able to see Jesus and his wounds with his own eyes. Thomas then believed. And so, after this if you doubted something, you were called a doubting Thomas.

Jesus *again* appeared eight days later, and said this to Thomas:

John 20:27 Then he said to Thomas, "Put your finger here, and see my hands; and put out your

hand, and place it in my side. Do not disbelieve, but believe."

John 20:28 Thomas answered him, "My Lord and my God!"

John 20:29 Jesus said to him, "Have you believed because you have seen me? Blessed are those who have not seen and yet have believed."

Jesus' brother James also struggled with belief. James chose not to follow his brother during the time that Jesus was alive. After all, this was his older brother. How could Jesus be anything out of the ordinary, especially the Messiah. Jesus' family actually thought he was crazy at one point and was going to take him away.

So, what changed their minds?

For one, they were amazed that Jesus had extraordinary powers to heal people and perform miracles. I mean... who can do that?

But, after knowing what Jesus had done while he was alive, and then witnessing Jesus' death and resurrection, James, in particular, was convinced that Jesus *was* the Christ. James became one of the leading proclaimers of Jesus and began to tell people that his brother was the Son of God... the Messiah they had been waiting for.

For more than 14 years, James was the head of the church in Jerusalem, and he no longer referred to Jesus as his brother but described himself as, a servant of the Lord Jesus Christ.

James 1:1 "James, a servant of God and of the Lord Jesus Christ"

The Jewish leaders were furious with James over the fact that he was converting people to follow Jesus. Subsequently, they killed him to shut him up in 62 AD.

Think about why James would choose to sacrifice his life for the brother he thought was a nobody all the time they were growing up. But, after reading the scriptures and witnessing the miraculous things his brother could do, his heart changed. He too now believed him to be the Messiah foretold to come.

Jesus' mother, Mary, always knew God was with her Son, and it was said that she pondered the many things Jesus did throughout his childhood in her heart.

Mary was also at Jesus' crucifixion along with the disciple John, witnessing the horrible things that were happening to him. And as Jesus hung on the cross, he asked John to look after his mother.

John 19:26-27 When Jesus saw his mother and the disciple whom he loved standing nearby, he said to his mother, "Woman, behold, your son!" Then he said to the disciple, "Behold, your mother!" And from that hour the disciple took her to his own home.

Now, because Jesus grew up in Nazareth, the Jewish leaders (Pharisees) also thought that he was born there as well. They knew from the scriptures that the Messiah must come from Bethlehem; which was indeed where Jesus was born. However, they didn't know this.

The Pharisees believed that Jesus threatened their religion, and that he was turning the people away from it. They were right.

The Jewish leaders were very concerned that Jesus' following was becoming too large. These leaders believed the Roman authorities would come down on the Jewish nation and then Pharisees would lose their positions of prominence. They were actually envious of His following.

Ultimately, Jesus would be killed for claiming to be the Son of God. Yet, he did not lie... HE <u>was</u> the Son of God.

But, back to Jesus' life. After becoming an adult, Jesus worked as a carpenter until the beginning of his public life, which was only three years in duration from the time he was thirty until thirty-three years old. In that short time, however, Jesus did incredible and miraculous things, and thousands upon thousands of people witnessed them.

It is very well documented that Jesus healed a great number of people and that he performed a staggering number of miracles; word of him quickly spread across the country. People travelled great distances to hear Jesus teach the Scriptures and be healed of their sicknesses and disease.

He drew such large crowds that twice, through miracles, he fed them before their long journey home because they had been with him for three days and he feared they would faint without food. It was reported that there were over five thousand men, plus women and children, on the first occasion, and over four thousand on the second occasion.

It's not like he could call the catering company and order food. They were in the middle of a deserted area. He called his Father instead, because with God, anything is possible.

When Jesus healed, the blind could see again and the crippled could now walk. Jesus also healed the deaf, the mute and every other ailment you could possibly think of, including bringing people back to life after they had died. Jesus was like no one else.

Who else can you name who has the power to do these things? No one has ever had the power to bring a person back from the dead… except for Jesus.

Nothing was too much for Him.

There has also never been anyone in the history of the world who has ever spoken with the authority that Jesus had. Jesus knew every scripture of the Old Testament, and constantly taught the people what they meant. He not only knew the entire Old Testament, but Jesus also reaffirmed the authority of it. He spoke to people all day long, telling them about His

Father, God, Heaven, and the reality of Hell. Jesus encouraged them to follow the Ten Commandments and obey God.

Jesus was kind, caring, and gentle, and did nothing wrong against God or the people.

The claims he made were clear, HE *was* the absolute fulfilment of the prophecies foretold in the Bible. **The entire Bible is about JESUS**. Period.

A modern day theologian explains it like this:

-In the Old Testament (a collection of ancient religious Hebrew writings by the Israelites): **Jesus is anticipated**

-In the Gospels (a theological explanation for the events in the life of Jesus of Nazareth): **Jesus is revealed to us**

-In the Book of Acts (the bridge between the Gospels and the Epistles): **Jesus is preached about**

-In the Epistles (letters to the early churches): **Jesus is explained**

I know this might seem like a long time ago and not relevant to today, yet, it is more relevant now than ever because we are nearing the time of Jesus' promised return.

Yes... Jesus, as well as the Bible, promises this event. Everything else in the Bible has come to pass, so why wouldn't this too?

Do you actually think this event will not happen just because *we* don't want to believe it?

Do you sincerely think we have more control than God? Don't be so foolish. We have been waiting two thousand years for this prophecy to come to pass, and if you compare the time of Jesus' birth with now, there also was a very long four hundred year 'time of silence' from God— like we have had in the past two thousand years.

However, even at that time, people who were faithful to the Scriptures, were ready and waiting for the Messiah (Jesus) to come.

God tells us the very same thing for this next time. Be ready.

Matthew 24:36 "But concerning that day and hour no one knows, not even the angels of heaven, nor the Son, but the Father only."

The Jewish people of that day were considered the most religious people of that time. You didn't dare break any of the religious rules for fear of being ousted from the synagogue, the Jewish house of worship. So, when Jesus began teaching about God and did not follow the traditional Jewish practice, the Pharisees, and Sadducees (the other religious leaders), became very angry and worried that people would start to follow Jesus instead of their religion. This worry consumed them and subsequently clouded their judgement.

If you look back to the time of Jesus, the early Jews were incredibly strict about their religion. They had made up many more rules inside of their religion to keep themselves 'clean' from sin. Pagan rules, man-made rules that were no longer of God, and because of these rules, the Jewish leaders refused to believe that Jesus was the Messiah.

However, the Jewish disciples of Jesus, on the other hand, were absolutely convinced that Jesus was in fact the Messiah. The ONE who was spoken about in the Old Testament.

Unfortunately, the Pharisees and Sadducees would not change their mind and accept who Jesus was.

Both the believers and non-believers in Jesus witnessed his miracles and saw, with their own eyes, people being healed. But the Jewish leaders were so caught up in their religion they could not see that this poor carpenter's son was in fact their saviour.

Yet, Jesus' disciples knew and believed. They couldn't help but follow Him. For them, believing in Jesus did not make their lives any easier, but they also could not deny that this was their Saviour. This was the Christ they had been waiting for and they would do anything to follow him.

Why would this small group of men who were Jesus' followers do this? Why would these men risk being kicked out of the synagogue, the sacred place of worship to God?

You must understand that it meant everything to be a part of the synagogue in those days. Men in that time wouldn't dare do anything outside of the Jewish laws that could affect their religious status. They had everything to lose.

But not only did these disciples follow Jesus, after he was crucified, these disciples were beaten, tortured, and killed because of their unwavering belief in him. Why on earth would they do that? Why would these men put themselves through this unbelievable agony to follow someone who was a fake?

These followers would never have done this unless they were completely convinced that Jesus was the Christ prophesied by God.

Consider the following scenario: Would you let yourself be beaten, tormented, and imprisoned simply because you believed something to be true? Or rather, would you risk being stoned to death or crucified for something you may or may not have believed to be true?

Obviously not. You'd never put yourself through something like that, you'd quit after the first beating. And even if you were confident, most of us would not suffer and die as a result.

These men, on the other hand, did this for the rest of their lives. Then, nearly all of them were martyred as a consequence for their belief in Jesus. Yet, most of us remarkably believe he was no one special.

These disciples also took the time to write many

letters after Jesus' death. The events the disciples witnessed impacted them immensely. Not only that, these men who suffered repeatedly for following Jesus, were inspired by God to write these letters so the details of his life and death would be known to all in the future.

Subsequently, those letters became extremely important. The writings of the disciples' eyewitness accounts later made up the books of the New Testament. I have no doubt that the impression these events had on their lives back then is comparable to those of us who were old enough to remember the moment of 9/11.

Think of how that event impacted us. The memory of 9/11 is still with us today, just as vivid as when it happened back in 2001.

Similarly, as to when Jesus performed his miraculous healings and rose from the dead. No one can do that... except Jesus, the Son of God.

Those historical events also left an impact on the people of that day who witnessed them, the same as 9/11 did for us.

When we look at the stories of Jesus told in the Bible, we know that they are rooted in history. Unlike the fables or legends passed down from generation to generation in many other religions. These Bible stories are factual eyewitness accounts that are told by first-hand witnesses of that time.

These biblical stories have also subjected

themselves extremely well to historical verification done by scholars who were both Christian and non-Christian. No one with any sense disputes the historical facts about Jesus Christ's life and death.

It has been proven that He was genuinely a real person who was crucified on a cross by the leaders of that day, and despite what we are led to believe, archaeologists, scientists, scholars, and historians back up the evidence of Jesus' life... and especially his death. There is also scientifically documented evidence of the earthquake at the time of Jesus' death

It's funny to think that Jesus' life and death stories prove to have much more fact-based evidence than any of the evolution stories scientists try to pass off as facts.

Here is another baffling thing to ponder. Let's think about time itself for a moment and presumably, this is something that has likely never crossed your mind.

Right now, we live in the year 2022 A.D. (Anno Domini), which is Latin for "The Year of the Lord."

So why does this matter, and what's the big deal?

Well… it is a HUGE deal, actually. If Jesus Christ, his death, and resurrection were insignificant, and Jesus was not who he said he was, then *why* did this monumental occasion of the start of the Gregorian Calendar happen at this very moment in time? Isn't it odd that this incredible man, Jesus, came on to the scene in the world the very same way the Jewish religious books predicted that he would, and then this man, Jesus, who was described as speaking with authority, like no one else ever had before, was witnessed demonstrating incredible powers, like no other man had before him.

These were not mere fables about him. Many people validated the miraculous healings that Jesus performed in front of HUGE crowds of people, and if this is in fact the truth (which it is), this should blow your mind!

Contemplate this as well. How do you explain how and why, as a result of Jesus' birth, the way we count time was changed and redefined?

For example, we say it is the year 2022, after Jesus' birth. Have you ever given this monumental occasion consideration? Why would the entire world stop the clock as they knew it, restart time at this unique moment in history, and then name the definition of time after this man?

That's an excellent question.

But after all, I'm sure Jesus wasn't THAT important. I mean… he was only a unique, perfect, sinless person who performed miracles we can't do, and completely changed the way we refer to time. But no big deal.

Yeah… I don't think so.

Also look at how we have altered the way we reference time before Jesus. We call it B.C. or before Christ. Historically anyone could have been chosen for a time altering event. So why this guy, Jesus, if he was a nobody?

When you deeply consider these facts alone, you have to ask... OK, why did this happen? Obviously, the impact of Jesus' short time here on earth was extremely important to humanity. No kidding.

However, this is the BIG question: Why did God send Jesus to us?

The simple answer is because we *require* a saviour in order to go to heaven. It's interesting that we all plan to go to heaven when we die, yet the Bible says we will not get there without Jesus. You NEED to know this!

Here's the thing: We are all sinners, especially me. Not one of us have obeyed God's commandments as we should have. Think of our time here on earth as a testing ground for loving and obeying God. Remember, God sent us His son, Jesus, to make us aware of our sins and to save us from hell. Loving Jesus is, for sure, a choice. No one is going to force you to love and obey God. That is why He gave us all free will to make our own decisions, much the same as Adam and Eve. They also had a choice. The Garden of Eden was humanity's first chance at heaven.

Believing in Jesus is our second chance... our last chance. God is far too loving to force us into going somewhere against our will.

Another fantastic Christian apologist I watch named Frank T., explains it in this way: "Say, there is a man who I do NOT care to date. But this man continues to pursue me to the point of being weird. This man is not at all deterred by my disinterest and says that he wants to force me into a relationship with him because he loves me so much. However, the feeling is not mutual."

Do you think because that man loves me this much, he can force me into a relationship with him? No, of course he can't. Love must be freely given and freely received.

This is the same with God. He sends us cards, letters, and flowers trying to convince us of his love, but God will NOT force us to love him. He knows that forcing us against our will does not work… we will be resentful. But because we have free will, we are also blessed with arrogance, and this arrogance enables us to think that we are 'super intelligent beings' who know everything.

We honestly believe that we don't need God's help. I am so guilty of this. But this is where God's Son comes into the picture. Jesus was sent as our redeemer, our second chance. No other person or religion has the power to save us, so do not let anyone try to tell you that there is some other way. There isn't… **only Jesus**.

<u>This</u> is **The Gospel of our Lord Jesus Christ.** The most IMPORTANT part of the Bible.

We have *all* sinned. There is not one of us who hasn't. God is not dumb; he knows this. But since we all have sinned, God sent his only Son, Jesus, to take the punishment for them. By God allowing Jesus to die on a cross and suffer immensely on our behalf, God can now forgive our sins.

But... there's a catch, and that catch is the choice we all must make.

It took me a long time to understand this, so I am trying to explain it as simply as I can, and in plain language. This is important!

Jesus taught, that in order for us to have eternal life in Heaven, we must repent and place our faith solely in HIM.

I'd say most people hear the word 'repent' and think, "Like... do I have to go see a priest?"

No, absolutely not! Repent means, "to ask forgiveness and change our ways." Stop doing the things that our conscience tells us are wrong. Pray and ask God to lead your life. He'll transform you into a completely different person, and as a result of that change, you will have no desire to engage in those actions that are considered sinful anymore.

You will not get to Heaven doing good deeds and praying repetitive prayers, no matter what your religion teaches you; only a personal relationship between you and Jesus will work. Jesus wants you to know him, and he wants to know you, similar to talking with a good friend. Tell God about your problems and ask him to help you and strengthen you.

It is so simple really. God hasn't made this complicated, we have.

As Ray Comfort. says, "Without Jesus as our saviour we should compare ourselves to people standing on the edge of a cliff without a parachute, and then we say to ourselves, when I fall, I will just flap my arms to save myself."

That's crazy, we cannot save ourselves without a parachute.

The same thing happens when we die, as much as we'd like to think we can, we cannot save ourselves. That parachute *is* Jesus, and the only way to God is THROUGH Jesus. How much more do I need to say to convince you of this?

Don't worry, I am going to say more.

I know that if you are hearing this for the first time, these words might confuse, surprise, or even offend you. But it is the TRUTH nonetheless, so please get right with God.

John 14:6 Jesus said to him, "I am the way, and the truth, and the life. No one comes to the Father except though me."

Jesus' disciple Peter, also said to the rulers in Jerusalem:

Acts 4:12 "And there is salvation in no one else, for there is no other name under heaven given among men by which we must be saved"

Ahh… but I hear you thinking, I am fine. We say to ourselves, "God is only for religious people.

I don't believe that Jesus is the only way to Heaven. I'll be OK."

As humans, we are educated, good people, and we do nice things. That doesn't matter. It won't work. Without the parachute, we die, and without our saviour, Jesus, the penalty of sin is death. It is either Heaven or Hell. There are no 'alternative' choices, and we will <u>not</u> be the decision makers at the time of judgement. GOD IS.

Romans 6:23 "For the wages of sin is death, but the free gift of God is eternal life in Christ Jesus our Lord."

However, because we love our sin, we don't care to hear God's words, so, we simply justify our infidelity and addiction to porn when we no longer feel a connection to our spouse. We also hold hatred in our hearts because we are too furious to forgive and have no qualms about lying to anyone in order to make ourselves appear to be great people. We then steal the things we desire because we want what other people have. It's not fair that we get the short end of the stick and have less than other people; whether it's their possessions or their way of life.

Well, the world is not fair unfortunately.

Yet, the most tragic sin towards God, is that we prefer to worship other faiths or false deities instead of Jesus, since they do not promise punishment and death for sins like he does.

There are definitely easier roads to follow, but are those roads worth it?

Hmmm... not when you know what is promised after we die. I mean, the Bible is very clear about Jesus' return and the coming judgement.

Why is it *so* difficult for us to accept God's word in the Bible and Jesus as our saviour? Is it because we didn't really know about Jesus before? Or maybe we simply haven't made the time to learn about Him.

I hope that is it. I hope you see how important your salvation is, and the salvation of your family as well, because nothing else in the world is as important as this.

Hell does not sound very pleasant, and I really don't want *any* of you to go there, so you need to figure this out and take the time to examine if I am telling the truth... sooner rather than later. Don't just take my word for it.

How do you know when it's your time to die? You don't. We occasionally get a heads-up, but most of the time we don't. In reality, waiting to be saved when you are older doesn't really work. Now is the time to sort out your eternity because it's too late after a head-on collision or a heart attack. You might not ever have another chance to make a choice at that moment.

Almost 6400 people in the world die every single hour. That's 106 people per minute.

Here's the mirror to use on Judgement Day. How

are you going to answer God when he asks if you have followed His commandments?

1) YOU SHALL HAVE NO OTHER GODS BEFORE ME
2) YOU SHALL NOT MAKE FALSE IDOLS
3) YOU SHALL NOT TAKE THE NAME OF THE LORD YOUR GOD IN VAIN
4) REMEMBER THE SABBATH DAY, KEEP IT HOLY
5) HONOUR YOUR FATHER AND MOTHER
6) YOU SHALL NOT MURDER
7) YOU SHALL NOT COMMIT ADULTERY
8) YOU SHALL NOT STEAL
9) YOU SHALL NOT BEAR FALSE WITNESS AGAINST THY NEIGHBOUR
10) YOU SHALL NOT COVET YOUR NEIGHBOUR

Could you imagine what a better place this world would be, if we had only followed these rules of God from the beginning? We wouldn't even need a court system.

God granted us free will to choose whether or not to accept his love. Since Adam and Eve failed at our first chance to be sinless, we now have to live in a fallen world until Jesus returns. This fallen world is hard to overcome because it contains so many desirable pleasures that we find difficult to say no to.

Fortunately, we have the advantage of a second chance. Satan wants us to be blissfully ignorant to what lies ahead if we don't choose Jesus during our lifetime. Don't let the last chance escape you because you assume you know better.

Please understand this.

Following Jesus is not the easy road to follow in this life. It is, without a doubt, the 'narrow road' talked about in the Bible. Don't get me wrong. I know how hard this road is, but I still choose to follow it because I see this road as the *only* path to heaven. The Bible tells us this over and over again... and so did Jesus.

Yes, the struggle to obey God is very real. God didn't hold any punches and told us that it would be difficult. But he also instructed us to **trust Him and fear not.** We live in a world filled with fear, and that fear is getting worse by the hour.

Here is the deal breaker that got to me. Why bother with any of this if we're only here for 75, 90, maybe a hundred years, and then we just fade to black after we die? No afterlife, no reckoning, no punishment for our behaviour. Who would care about anything? Simply generate as much wealth as you can, buy nice stuff, and have a good time while you're here.

This is how *most* of us think and live our lives, without a clear understanding of what is to come.

However, just think: If God is serious about punishing sinners (and He is), and he means eternal life after we die (which He does), then that would mean forever and ever.

Not a hundred years, not a thousand years, but millions, billions, and trillions of years. Maybe we should seriously consider believing in Jesus if it means our only two choices are either Heaven or Hell for eternal life.

Think about the term 'eternity' for a moment. Our intelligent minds cannot even contemplate that length of time. All we know is a hundred years... and we think that's a long time.

No, it's not. Eternity is a long time. So, the next place is far more important than this one.

For me, it is not even a question of which way to go. I know full well that our modern society does not like God, the Bible, or Jesus. I also know that I will most certainly have to deal with hatred, cancel culture, and the loss of some friends and family.

Yet what is that in exchange for an eternal life of joy versus an eternal life of suffering if the word of God is correct. We will all have to make this choice, and I cannot make the choice for anyone else. All I can do is try to convince you to look at the facts and plant a seed.

Death comes to all of us eventually, so for me, the hard road suddenly doesn't seem so hard when you compare it to the alternative end destination. It is definitely not worth the risk of being wrong about this and continually living life like there is no one to answer to, or living as if there is no place of eternity where our souls will be forever and ever.

If I'm wrong, oh well, I guess I missed out on some theft or using lies to enhance my work situation and make more money. I'm certain I also missed out on some really wild parties.

But, and here's the big BUT... if *you* are wrong, you are promised an eternal Hell.

Jesus described hell many times in the Bible and used words such as, "where there is fire and gnashing of teeth" and "eternal agony."

Matthew 13:41-42 "The Son of Man will send his angels, and they shall gather out of his kingdom all causes of sin and all law-breakers, and will throw them into the fiery furnace. In that place there will be weeping and gnashing of teeth."

When we hear this reality of judgement, we assume God doesn't love us. But honestly, it is the total opposite. God <u>deeply</u> loves us and does not want any of us to go to hell because every single person is important to God. Hell was supposed to be a place for Satan, not us.

However, we too will go there if we choose to follow Satan instead of God.

Why such harsh punishment? Most of us would say, "We haven't been terrible people, we don't deserve this."

Our biggest problem is that we are using our *own* standards, not God's. If we punish a child for not listening or a criminal for breaking the law, we can justify the punishment because of humanities standard of good. Yet, God's standard is way more 'just' and 'holy' than ours based on the Ten Commandments.

Do we follow them? Well, we try… but not really.

Why do we feel that we can do whatever we please without having to answer to anyone when we die? We can't do that in this world right now. So, if God is our creator (which He is), why does this punishment seem harsh? It's not.

Why do we continue to think God is not serious, or that there is no God?

I suppose the answer is because we feel no one truly knows.

Well... I know. I am absolutely certain. I have read his word, prayed and talked with Him. I know that God is there. He is the reason I am writing this book. We are so willfully ignorant, don't give up your eternity because of your arrogance today. This almost happened to me. God is extremely patient, loving, and kind, and gives us so many chances to change our ways.

Jesus tried very hard to convince the Pharisees of his day to change their ways and trust in him. Many of them didn't. The Jewish leaders believed that they knew God better than Jesus. They also weren't convinced that Jesus was the Messiah because they did not know the scriptures.

Even today, many Jewish people are waiting for the Messiah to show up, but as the world becomes increasingly more like what God has foretold in the 'end times,' more and more Jewish people are now seeing that Jesus *was* the Saviour.

In the Bible, Jesus tells us a story about two men. I say, 'in the Bible', but Jesus actually taught these lessons to people in person. The New Testament part of the Bible was written after he died, so yes, in the

Bible, but the words came from the real man who was a fantastic storyteller. Jesus often used stories (parables) to help people relate to what he was teaching.

The story Jesus told of the two men goes like this: Lazarus was a man who loved God even though he was extremely poor and very hungry. He suffered every day with sores on his body outside the gate of a rich man, longing to be fed by the crumbs that fell from the rich man's table. Then Lazarus died, and he went to heaven.

The other man, the rich man who did not obey God's word, also died, and was cast into hell. The rich man cried out from hell, and said:

Luke 16:24 "Father Abraham, have mercy on me, and send Lazarus to dip the end of his finger in water and cool my tongue, for I am in anguish in this flame."

Understand that this rich man believed that <u>he</u>, not Lazarus, was going to heaven. The rich man believed this because he strictly followed his religion and did good things, so he was destined for heaven. Besides, he was wealthy, proud, and lived a good life.

However, instead of listening to what the prophecies said in the scripture, he pushed aside God's word and didn't accept them. He thought he knew better than God... kind of like most of us today.

Only after realizing that he was now in hell for eternity, the rich man asked Abraham to send someone to his brothers who were still alive, to warn them.

Abraham (who was an Old Testament patriarch) replied and said to him, if his brothers didn't believe while living on earth with the amount of evidence given in the Old Testament scriptures, neither would they believe if a messenger was sent to them.

And so here was the rich man. In this place of eternal torment, knowing it was too late for him to be saved... harsh, I know, but it is not too late for you.

I know what you're thinking... because I also reasoned the same thing in my own mind. You're asking, "What kind of God would do this?" What kind of loving God would send us to Hell and torment us? I'm sure this is the one question that most people can't get past, and honestly, it took me a long time as well. Only now, after knowing and loving God and Jesus, can I truly tell you the answer; a 'just' and 'holy' God who promises those who refuse to obey him.

We haven't given God any other choice but to separate the unrepentant people from *His* goodness. This is our own decision, so remember that fact. If it were up to God, we would *all* choose him.

We are God's children. Every one of us. How would we respond to a child that refuses to listen thinking that, they (the child), knows better than the parent? Would we reward that child for not following the rules? No, of course we wouldn't.

As a result of our decisions, God, like any good judge, will punish those who refuse to obey his rules. After all, HE is our creator and can do what he wants.

What we fail to realize if we choose to worship evil instead of God after he has been so patient with us, is that God will have no choice but to separate us from him.

I know, I hear you thinking. You are saying, "This is crazy, I don't believe this."

However, I'll say it again. Just because you say you don't believe it, does not mean it is not going to happen. God promises a 'Day of Judgement' for all people, and not one person will escape it. Not even one.

Jesus called the most religious people of his day 'snakes and vipers', and those religious people were the church leaders; the ones who thought they were the closest to God. Jesus was trying to get the point across to them that they were wrong in trusting in their own ability to go to heaven. Think about that.

Here's an analogy for you.

If a court judge said to you, "Bob, I find you guilty of your crime and I am sentencing you to death with the electric chair."

And you say, "Well judge, listen… here's the thing, I actually don't believe in the electric chair."

Will your unbelief change the outcome? Exactly...

So, arrogant denial will not work. Unbelief will

not work. Cancel culture will not work. Do your due diligence, my friends, and find the answer to this yourself.

And if you are feeling convicted of sin and assuming it is too late for you, PLEASE do not lose hope. God is very gracious, loving, and patient. No matter what you have done, or how many times you've broken the commandments, God will <u>always</u> forgive you right up to the time of Jesus' return. But understand this; there is a cut-off day. Prepare for your eternity now. We have no idea when this day of judgement, or the day of our death will come.

Matthew 7:23 "And then I will declare to them, 'I never knew you; depart from me, you workers of lawlessness."

It is so simple in reality, but we have allowed so much doubt into our lives, whether through life experiences or our educational systems. We also doubt because we perceive ourselves as 'worldly' and 'intelligent'. Our arrogance has literally cast the most doubt in our minds, and that doubt fuels the reason why we have so much trouble comprehending God's greatness, his words, and his plan... because <u>we</u> think we are so great.

In our own humanist rationalism, we reason to ourselves that there is absolutely no way this stuff will ever happen. Don't be so sure. It would be foolish of you to not find the answer to this question to satisfy any doubt that you might have. We are only going to get one shot at dying.

Yet, deep down, I think we all know there is a God. It has only been in the last one hundred and fifty years that we have questioned if there actually is.

I'll say it again, Jesus spoke of hell many, many times. But He spoke of it to warn people and used the ugliness of hell as a motivating factor to keep us out of there. In our worldview, it seems that proof of everything is required, especially in order to have a belief in God.

Even if we consider our current life, we believe in all sorts of things we can't see. Things such as love, gravity, electricity, and the assurance that evolution is a fact. Just a reminder... it is not.

Why do we not think an all-Creator God doesn't have the ability to make sense of this world? What kind of incredibly miraculous circumstances had to happen for this wonderful creation called Earth to exist? When we try to reason it inside of our world view, we become confused because what we only know for certain is what is here and now.

In the meantime, we blatantly ignore the fact that everything we see can be explained through Creation and God, in the Bible.

Believe me. All I am aiming to do is help you see things through a different lens. The Bible is the only thing that actually explains our being here and is also the only thing that makes sense of the world we have today.

It is all in there.

It is so much easier NOT to be a Christian, and it would be far simpler to just go with the flow of the common world view, but this is why Jesus talked so much about the narrow gate. He knew things would get tough for believers.

He said:

Matthew 7:13-14 "Enter through the narrow gate. For wide is the gate and broad is the road that leads to destruction, and many enter through it. For the gate is narrow and the way is hard that leads to life, and those who find it are few."

People often refuse God because of our problem with pride. We find ourselves going along with the masses, doing the same as everyone else while making excuses for our tolerance towards sin. The broad and easy road doesn't require much of a moral standard, and it certainly doesn't require any commitment or sacrifice. We can be self-indulgent and permissive on the wide road, doing whatever we want and using our own standards of judgment. This is the broad road, the easy road. Most people will choose *this* path.

Jesus said this:

Luke 13:24 "Strive to enter through the narrow gate, for many, I say to you, will seek to enter and will not be able."

If you are unwilling to trust in Jesus, he says the cost is great. We can't take our baggage of materialism and sin with us through the narrow gate.

Actually, we can't take anything with us to the afterlife. So, then, why is our stuff so important to us?

If we were to become terminally ill tomorrow, would we say, "I need to go use my stuff before it's too late?"

Or would we instead say, "Please pray for me?"

Please… I'm encouraging you, strive for the narrow gate. Do something difficult in this life to preserve your life everlasting. I can guarantee you, that if you ask Jesus to help you with a surrendered heart, he will absolutely help you on this journey.

Last question. Was Jesus lying when he said there is a Heaven and a Hell? Jesus talked about Hell over seventy times in his short time of teaching here on Earth.

It is also well documented that Jesus did not lie… even once. ***Think about that…***

Chapter Eight
The Promised Places

"And do not fear those who kill the body but cannot kill the soul. Rather fear him who can destroy both soul and body in hell."
Matthew 10:28

Heaven and Hell. These two words have either grabbed your attention, or you are closing the pages of this book.

Have these two supposed mythical places been told as stories throughout the generations, or is there some real evidence for them?

Regardless, this is probably one of the most important topics that you will ever learn about in your life because you certainly don't want to end up in one of these afterlife places.... namely Hell.

I find most people do not want to converse about either one, but we definitely prefer not to discuss Hell. The reason we don't care to talk about either is that if we don't discuss them, no one will convince us that they are real, and if we don't accept that they are real, we can simply keep carrying on as we normally would without a thought of them. So, it's easier to just cancel them.

I'm certain all of us wonder if Hell is an actual place. I mean... ya, it's not somewhere we want to believe is real because it's quite frightening if you seriously think about it. But what I suspect really motivates us to avoid the topic is the thought of Hell being the place where we could truly end up when we die, and who wants to dwell on that. Certainly not me.

However, the more information I consumed about this topic, the more it seemed like Hell was going to be *my* afterlife reality.

I was indeed a sinner. It was the realization that I had not obeyed God that scared me to the point of panic. I was terrified and the thought of literally 'going to Hell' encouraged me to pursue answers to the questions that most of us desire to avoid.

It really is an illusion to reject something just because we do not believe it. Things simply do not go away because we choose not to believe them. We try, but it doesn't work.

So, how valid are the words written in the Bible about Hell? I definitely had to search for the truth about this; and after much reading, I was amazed at the conclusion I came to.

Let's begin by defining what Hell is— and what it isn't.

According to the Bible, I don't think Heaven and Hell are anything like what we have depicted them to be. In this life, the Devil, Lucifer, or Satan, is usually portrayed as a 'fictional' character that we often make light of. We are smacked with images of a man in a red suit, with black hair and horns coming out of his head, who has a pointy black beard, and often sporting a red cape. This false image is sometimes emphasized by a long-spaded tail, tipped ears, and a very sharp pointed trident (pitchfork).

You would envision this depiction as a cartoon 'Halloween' type of impression of the Devil, and even though this describes a visual perception of evil really well, this is not the Satan or Devil that is spoken about in the Bible.

In reality, Satan is a sophisticated, smooth, and sly demonic spirit who is often described in the Bible as the lawless one, the ultimate deceiver, or shrewd liar. He is way more intelligent and deceiving than most of us give him credit for, and he heavily influences nasty behaviour in our society.

There is no hiding the fact that Satan has a very firm grip on this world and is in charge of the demonic evil happening today because God gave the world over to him after Adam and Eve disobeyed him.

Satan is definitely the ringleader of the evil we

have experienced in the past, and, as foretold, we see evil increasing dramatically and rapidly in the world today.

Sometimes that evil is in very blatant ways, but not always. Often, Satan's agenda is advanced through subtleties that are slipped into culture, such as the de-sensitizing of society. For many years, Satan has been conditioning us to accept things that God told us are unacceptable.

Notice today what is now considered mainstream and acceptable in the world and compare it to only a few decades ago. It's unbelievable how much more evil we have become in such a short amount of time, and how much more we now tolerate because we think God is no big deal.

I know most of us also struggle to keep up with all the dishonesty going on. It inundates our social media apps and television. We often wonder how people can act in such a way, but then in the next moment, we become aware of an even worse evilness, and it sets the new bar for desensitizing the shock value for us humans. As we witness more and more evil, it just becomes the new normal and we are virtually helpless to do anything about it.

Even more disturbing, however, are the increasing crimes against our children, such as child abuse, pornography, and child sexual abuse. We have almost totally lost all morality within society.

Who in their right mind... and I use that word

loosely, could do such things to innocent little humans for their own pleasure? Only someone who is led by absolute evilness could comprehend doing such terrible things to children. And even though the majority of us are not regularly exposed to this perverted and twisted version of humanity, it is happening more frequently than ever before all across this planet.

The worst part being that the darkness of these individuals and groups is not only led by non-religious people, but a good portion of the abuse also comes from a form of religion.

It is so screwed up! God help us.

In my opinion, a very large portion of the world's population do not make a conscious effort to learn about Hell. I mean, after all, Hell sounds ridiculous. Why would anyone believe it?

As humans, we also reason to ourselves that if Hell is true, it would simply be unfair for God to send us there.

But let me tell you what Hell really is. Hell is the place that God warns us about in the Bible. In fact, during Jesus' three years of ministry, he spoke of Hell more often than he did of Heaven and described it very vividly, time and time again, constantly warning us of what is to come.

He described it as being a place of everlasting torment... not torture, but torment, where it will be impossible to give or receive joy and love. A place where we will lose everything that we know is pleasurable. There will be zero relationships in Hell.

I know... you thought you were going to meet your buddies there for a party, but sorry, that's not happening.

Hell is promised to bring us pure despair. A place where we will experience everlasting anguish and regret, and our comfort is professed to be stripped away... forever.

Think about the word 'forever' for a moment. We actually have no idea what it means.

No, it's not seventy to ninety years, that would be difficult enough, but the promise of forever means millions, billions, and trillions of years of eternal suffering. And, once we are there, there is no turning back.

I'm not sure about you, but that is completely terrifying to me.

So why is Hell a place? If God is so good and he made all the people, why would there be this other terrifying place?

Like I said before, Hell is for Satan and his evil demon angels as a place to be separated from good. Again, this place was not intended for us, but unfortunately, if we decide to follow evil instead of God's goodness, we too will go there.

Keep in mind, however, that the God who sends us to this Hell is the same God who sent His only Son, Jesus, to be tortured by people and die for our sins in order to keep us *out* of Hell.

The ball is totally in our court. We can not blame God for our choices.

This is where 'free will' comes back into the big picture. It is our absolute right to choose what we believe. But one thing is for certain, and we keep forgetting this, we will all die someday. Every single one of us will be held accountable for our choices, and some of us will be punished forever. In that promised punishment, there is absolutely nothing you can ransom for another chance of Heaven at that point... it will be too late.

There is also no way to avoid God's judgement and you cannot wish it away. He promises that every one of us will be judged because in his infinite wisdom and holiness, God must give us our due reward.

Think about it. What society would choose not to have a justice system?

It is the same for God.

If you... in your lifetime, have heard the **Good News of Jesus** (the Gospel), and you refuse to do anything with it because of your pride or arrogance, you will stand convicted on judgement day. That day is promised to be a day of darkness and light where some will experience a second death. Perhaps it will be the day of death for your God-created soul.

And again, I repeat, I don't understand why we think God would not do what he has promised to do. He has made good on all his other promises. This *should* get your attention. You have a choice.

Remember, the Bible states that, "the wages of sin, is death." That death in sin is promised in the description of Hell, but eternal life is also available and promised in the description of Heaven.

Romans 6:23 "For the wages of sin is death; but the gift of God is eternal life through Jesus Christ our Lord"

It's funny to think… maybe 'funny' is not a good choice of word, but as a matter of fact, in this life we make such light of Hell. We tell people to 'go to hell' and say, 'what the hell'. We also listen to songs such as ACDC's 'Highway to Hell' and celebrate the lyrics with drinking and dancing. However, there is no 'crazy awesome fun party' planned there, so don't be fooled.

The Bible also names Hell as a place called 'Shoel' or 'Hades,' which means "a place of darkness or a permanent place of the dead."

You're probably thinking, "Well then, if it is a place of the dead... and I'm dead, I won't feel a thing. So, what would it matter if Hell is actually real?"

Unfortunately, that's not what the Bible teaches. The torment of your soul is the eternal punishment that is promised for refusing to accept the amazing gift that God offers you.

In Hell, we are cut off from everything good and separated from God FOREVER.

So, what about this great place called Heaven. No… I don't see it as being a place with constant harps or us floating on clouds.

So, what then will it be?

In the Bible, Heaven is described as a place of complete peace and rest. Not the same peace we know here, but an unexplainable peace that we have never experienced before.

How many of us have true peace in our lives right now? I'm sure not many of us do, because this world doesn't cater to peace. Most of us can't even begin to comprehend what the peace of Heaven would even feel like. This world is so chaotic and angry.

However, Heaven will be exactly as God intended it to be. A place of no more sickness or disease, and no more pain and suffering. God promises to wipe away all our tears and sorrows, and most certainly, evil will no longer be any part of God's new world.

That is not all the good stuff.

We are promised feasts and celebrations with vineyards and fruit, plus all the things we enjoy now will be a thousand times better in Heaven. It is so hard to imagine all this wonderfulness because this world is all we know. No one will know this for certain until it happens, but this is what God promises us. So, if we believe in God, we must also believe what he promises, even if it appears impossible to us.

In our worldly minds, we reason to ourselves that there is no way this could ever happen, but God asks us to trust Him, believe, and fear not.

I'm also guessing, like me, you probably find yourself thinking sometimes, "Do I really want to keep living forever?"

This life can be so mundane, and we believe it will be the same in the next life. But the Bible doesn't say that at all. It talks about us having things to do in heaven. The difference will be that the work in heaven is promised to not be a burden like it is in today's world.

In Heaven, we will inhabit God's house and be in the presence of God with new bodies that do not decay. We will also be reunited with family, friends, sons and daughters; the ones who we have lost in this world, who also believed and trusted in Christ.

Yet, I believe that the most exciting thing God promises us is that the innocent people of this world will be in heaven as well, such as the mentally challenged, the young, and babies who have been born... and the unborn. Those who were not given the opportunity to choose Christ.

Yet I know you will ask this tough question, "What about those people whom we dearly loved, but did not make a decision to accept Jesus?"

I realize that this is so difficult for us to comprehend, but God promises we will not be sad about them in Heaven.

I know. This might sound terrible at first because how could we not remember them? Honestly though, think about how real joy and rest could be possible if we kept thinking of loved ones who made their own choice not to choose God. There is nothing we can do for them at this point because in life, God will have given them many chances to choose him.

But you can certainly do something now to help them... encourage them to choose Jesus.

In Heaven, God also promises that the 'curse of death' will be no more and that we will never be tired or weary. Only filled with joy. How amazing is that?

God created us with three distinct parts, our body, our spirit, and our soul. God loves all of us, but especially our souls. It is who we are. God created us as individuals, and each one of us is distinct from one another with our own thoughts, minds, and souls. We are not identical mechanical beings.

He also expects us to take care of our bodies. Our body is not merely a vessel for our soul, it is an absolute wonder that was also assembled by God. Treat it well.

In Heaven, our souls are promised to be reunited with our new bodies, never to die again. And when we are in Heaven, for the first time ever, we will be fully aware of the being of love, named God. It doesn't get much better than that.

It is summarized like this: God did not intend for his world to be full of corruption and violence, but after the corruption and sin started, God had a plan.

Yes, God created us. Yes, he should have known that corruption was going to happen because he created us. We can never know for certain why things happened as they did. But I repeat, what is not fully understood by many people is that God also created us with free will. You are probably getting tired of me saying this.

God also takes no pleasure in the death of sinners, yet, he will also never force someone into his presence against their will.

In this life, if someone denies God's power and says, "No God, not your will, but my will," don't you think our God is loving enough to say, "As you wish then, *your* will be done."

All we want as humans is the power to make up our own minds— and God knows this.

As I said before, you cannot pay someone to fall in love with you, just as God will not force someone to love him. In these modern days of personal choice and freedom to choose, we should all understand this. It is our choice to love and follow Him... or not. Freedom to choose is a necessary condition for love.

One last thing to think about.

In our lifetime (meaning most of us born in the twentieth and twenty-first centuries), more humans have died at the hands of other humans than at any other time in recorded history.

Now, this should really upset us... and change us. But we are not getting any less violent, and we are certainly not getting any more kind. No matter how much we should have learned from our past, we are still becoming more and more evil.

Why is this?

If this fact upsets us, how do you think God feels? Is God not supposed to deal with this incredibly powerful human evilness?

So, if Heaven exists, and we all believe we're going there, ***why wouldn't we think there might be a Hell too?*** Good question...

Chapter Nine
The Cool Kids

"Be sober-minded; be watchful. Your adversary the devil prowls around like a roaring lion, seeking someone to devour."
1 Peter 5:8

New Age Spiritualism has become increasingly popular around the world and is clearly the new trendy religion that is very open-minded. It's no wonder why so many people are flocking to it in the modern age we are in. But, as society becomes less attracted to God, this is no coincidence.

For starters, it is much easier to be spiritual than it is to be Christian or Religious. Unlike religions, spiritualism has no central scriptures. It is organized, but informal and very disparate; and there is no specific doctrine to follow— it is very 'fluid.'

Spirituality, also known as New Age, is defined

as a designer spiritual practice that allows people to shape their beliefs to fit whatever parameters they perceive. Therefore, their spirituality can perfectly suit their worldview, especially when there is no specific stance on any issues. As a result, spiritualism remains neutral in order to not offend anyone.

The dictionary describes Spiritualism as, "a belief that spirits of the dead communicate with the living, usually through a medium."

Seemingly, spiritualism promotes the use of spiritual guides, such as angels or spirit beings because, intuitively, humans have a genuine need to be connected to something spiritual.

Studies have shown that people tend to feel better about life when they have the feeling of a spiritual presence around them. This is another reason why spiritualism has become a very seductive practice.

Spiritualism also promises to give us hope of an afterlife and can best be described as a belief that seeks something mystical or unknown in the hope that there is indeed something bigger than us.

But unfortunately, being spiritual is not recognized in the Bible as a path to everlasting life in Heaven.

Right away... I know what you're thinking. "Who cares *what* the Bible says if I'm happy in my own spiritualism?"

I hear you, but this is important. What if you're unknowingly on the wrong path that is leading you somewhere other than Heaven? Wouldn't you want to know?

Know this also... it is NEVER my intention to offend anyone. I am not stating these words for any other reason than to make you aware of what the Bible teaches about these topics. Society has disregarded the Bible so much that most of us won't even take the time to look into it.

However, the truth is far more important to hear than someone telling you what you want to hear.

So why is New Age not the right path? If you think about Spiritualism, it is an individualized style of faith where believers are not held accountable for anything. It works on the basis of relative truth, such as, "What's true for me doesn't have to be true for you."

There is no such thing as 'your truth' in anything. It does not exist. *Your truth* simply means that people are relying on their own impressions or opinions. Just because someone believes something to be true, it doesn't mean that it is true for everyone else.

Ahh, but I hear you thinking again.

You say, "What are you telling me? Isn't this your opinion because you believe the Bible to be true?"

Well, no... actually.

The Bible *is* the truth of God. This is the **true** truth (absolute truth). I have been wrong about my truth (my opinion) many times and have had to go back to the Bible to correct my truth, back to God's truth. I don't ever want to rely on what I think is true anymore. God's truth is all that matters, especially if he's the one who has made all of this possible... and us. We aren't the truth creators... GOD is.

In your own reasoning, if you conclude that your relative truth is OK as long as your thoughts or beliefs do not cause pain or harm to someone else, I would ask you, "OK for whom?"

A world without moral rules does not bode well for anyone. Your relative truth might be something totally different from what society on the whole deems as a general moral standard.

Do we continue to quietly move the standard until it suits everyone? It's like saying, "I am going to make my own rules... and you make yours."

Well, that's great and all... until your rules conflict with someone else's rules. In reality, this does not work. This is why humanity has a standard set of rules to begin with.

Here is what Spiritualism, or New Age, teaches. Generally, Spiritualism focuses on *this* life. The here and now. New Age mostly rejects 'mono-theism', meaning that their belief system does not accept a single creator God. But if a spiritual movement happens to teach a one-God theology, then 'the god' figure is usually described as a higher power or natural force, not as the Creator God.

Spiritualism also encourages us to emit 'good vibes' and 'good energy' toward other people. How exactly do you do that? We can't even make a single grain of sand with all the technology we have, so how could we possibly think that we can emit enough good vibes to help someone?

I think we often confuse the expression of good energy, with having a good attitude. Rather than 'thinking' something such as a good vibe, the action of a good attitude allows us to be physically helpful and kind to people. This is God's attitude.

Thinking good energy is useless… and offers no help or commitment from the thinker. It *is* much easier, however.

Leviticus 19:31 "Give no regard to mediums and familiar spirits; do not seek after them, to be defiled by them. I am the LORD your God."

New Age constantly uses terms such as inclusiveness, self-love, awareness, rediscovery, positivity, affirmation, channeling, visualization, and self-acceptance, among many more. It focuses on belief in yourself, not belief in God.

Spiritualism also practices many rituals, such as the Law of Attraction, Ouija (wee gee) boards, karma, reiki, tantra, and… yes, I'm sorry to say, even yoga.

Please understand that I am <u>not</u> saying there is anything wrong with the exercise portion of yoga. The problem lies within the yoga salutations. Salutations are used as spiritual healing techniques in New Age Spiritualism in order to get closer to the spirit world.

"So, what is wrong with that?" you ask.

Well… for one, it encourages people to bow down

to other 'gods' and then puts their trust and belief in those practices opening the door for the evil realm.

Now, this is not a problem if you have *no* desire to go to Heaven.

However, if you *do* wish to go to Heaven, these things are for sure a problem. A HUGE problem.

These are not innocent actions, doing no harm as we are led to believe. These kinds of rituals elevate you or another deity to the status of 'a god', and the God who actually created you doesn't appreciate this.

New Age followers also seek assistance from material objects, such as obtaining healing energy from crystals or sage burning.

Alternatively, they may also request guidance from other sources through fortune telling or horoscopes, hoping for signs from a spiritual being to lead them through life.

But we are not 'winners' who can rely solely on ourselves to overcome life's challenges. Only God has the ability to conquer evil. Until you fully understand this fact, you will not even realize that spiritualism is contrary to the commandments laid out in the Bible— by the real God.

The result of allowing these demonic forces into our lives encourages the demonic dimension to take control of us, allowing other spiritual entities to infiltrate our souls.

This isn't to say, that you'll go out and do things that are considered evil in this world, but it will definitely push you further away from God. Once you've entered that realm of doubt and scepticism toward God, the wicked one will fight hard to keep you there.

Remember, Satan's purpose is to obscure your understanding of the one who created us (God), and then he imprisons us in that false belief system in order to capture your soul into his everlasting darkness.

The Bible's second commandment encourages us to love and trust the creator God alone. This battle for our souls is unquestionably a spiritual battle fought on a level far beyond our comprehension.

Keep an eye on what's going on in the world right now.

2 Corinthians 11:14-15 "And no wonder, for even Satan disguises himself as an angel of light. So it is no surprise if his servants, also, disguise themselves as servants of righteousness."

I know instinctively in my soul that no one believes 'we humans' are just a bunch of atoms floating around. If indeed the spiritual realm exists, and God exists, and you imply your own set of rules to that realm, you are essentially molding your own beliefs to suit *your* spiritual world view, not God's. Once you've chosen not to follow God and instead follow whatever spiritualism promises you, you've essentially joined forces with Satan, because God is the only other option.

I honestly believe spiritualists are searching

for a 'jesus' of sorts and aren't even aware of what danger they are in. They are looking for something or someone who can give them hope for a peaceful existence beyond death.

However, Satan, the ultimate deceiver, gets in the way of us experiencing God's true peace by convincing us that we can get what we need through other means, such as spirituality.

I absolutely understand how difficult these words are to hear. They are, nevertheless, crucial to comprehend before you arrive at your eternal home. You do not want to be mistaken in this.

1 John 4:1 "Beloved, do not believe every spirit, but test the spirits to see whether they are from God, for many false prophets have gone out into the world."

Not too surprisingly, there are also many famous people who promote New Age theology, and some of them disguise it as a form of Christianity— but with more tolerance.

One of these famous people is everyone's favourite talk show host with dark curly hair. Everyone likes her. She is successful, she's rich, she does nice things... and she also believes there are multiple ways to get to Heaven. You'll make more friends this way.

This talk show host promotes a 'prosperity gospel' in which you are encouraged to believe that <u>you</u> are in full control, and that it is not necessary to obey all those *harsh* words in the Bible because she promises that you have the authority to pick and choose the words you like— the ones that you can live with. Easy peasy.

To her, God is an impersonal force... a conscious, universal energy. Sound familiar?

She not only dismisses Jesus' teachings in the Bible, but she has also promoted New Age beliefs for twenty-five years along with her super wealthy prosperity church friends.

She is most definitely, NOT a Christian.

1 Timothy 4:1-2 "Now the Spirit expressly says that in later times some will depart from the faith by devoting themselves to deceitful spirits and teachings of demons, through the insincerity of liars whose consciences are seared,"

Many of these new, progressive, far-left, so-called 'Christian' churches have found their way into western society. These churches advocate far-left agendas rather than standard conservative views. Some of them sincerely believe Jesus was just a man, resulting in a twisting the words of God in these New Age style churches to promote socialism and prosperity for all.

Don't get sucked in by it. They are counterfeit Christian churches that seek to appease the preferences of our modern religious culture rather than God.

In this way, however, no one who attends this

style of church is offended, or offends anyone else…
EXCEPT for the true God they seek to worship.

Spiritualism has certainly transferred power to the people, which is fantastic for humanity's perceived freedom, but it violates everything that God has taught us. Our issue is that we are uninterested in admitting our faults, and if we don't have to face them, they will simply disappear. We are unquestionably witnessing the genuine love of God being purged of anything that makes people feel uncomfortable. It's unbelievable actually.

It is described in the Bible as follows:

2 Timothy 4:3-4 "For the time is coming when people will not endure sound teaching, but having itching ears, they will accumulate for themselves teachers to suit their own passions, and will turn away from listening to the truth and wander off into myths."

1 John 1:8 "If we say that we have no sin, we deceive ourselves, and the truth is not in us."

This verse talks about God's Holy Spirit:

John 16:13 "When the Spirit of truth comes, he will guide you into all truth, for he will not speak on his own authority, but whatever he hears he will speak, and he will declare to you the things that are to come."

I think sometimes people seek spiritualism as an alternative to dealing with the fact that death seems final. We fear death because we are born only knowing life, so we live our lives with the constant dread of death. It scares us… and so it should.

The Devil will grant you all kinds of things in this life in order to entice you because he would rather you spend eternity in his place. Unwillingly, you are trading a temporary benefit in this world for a place of eternal peace with God.

Deeply think this through. What *if* what I am telling you is true? What *if* spiritualism is a path to Hell after you die? What *if* you knew for certain that following Spiritualism would lead you to torment and anguish in the afterlife? Would that change your belief?

Eternal peace is a gift from God. It is the reward he gives you after you die for trusting and believing in Jesus Christ. We all need peace, and I know in my heart that the people seeking New Age religions are only seeking peace as well, but they are being duped into believing that it is all about us and this life. That's a lie, it is not.

2 Peter 2:1 "But false prophets also arose among the people, just as there will be false teachers among you, who will secretly bring in destructive heresies, even denying the Master who bought them, bringing upon themselves swift destruction."

It's also concerning that spirituality frequently involves the use of psychedelics or hallucinogenic drugs to induce a non-ordinary state of consciousness. These hallucinogens heighten spiritual experiences by putting you in a euphoric state of illusion.

When you achieve an 'aura' state of harmony through the use of these hallucinogens, you can then trigger the six levels of chakra, with the greatest stage being the 'third eye'— also known as the inner mind. It is thought that when this eye is opened, a completely new realm of reality is revealed.

This is the absolute worship of evil because anything outside of the worship of God is wicked.

What does New Age Spiritualism promise you in the afterlife that is so great? Good question.

Spiritualism can be defined as beliefs and practices that attempt to bring a person into a harmonious relationship with a sacred realm or being. I think the key word here is 'attempt'.

As I have said before, I believe New Agers are seeking a spiritual realm to help them cope... just not the one of Jesus Christ or God. Because as sinful humans, we don't like what God has to say, or what he stands for. We also do not like being convicted of what we are doing wrong, especially if we believe that we are doing everything right and being a good person.

But, if God is real (which he is), and heaven and hell are real (which they are), these two realities become very important— the most important things you will ever learn.

A famous atheist magician once said something like this: "How much do you have to hate someone to not proselytize (tell them about God)? How much do you have to hate somebody to believe that everlasting life is possible and not tell them that? I mean, if I believed beyond the shadow of a doubt and knew that a truck was bearing down on you, and you didn't believe that the truck was actually bearing down on you, there's a certain point where I tackle you to save you... and <u>this</u> is way more important than that."

This certainly <u>is</u> more important than that. I believe, beyond the shadow of a doubt, that the truck is bearing down on you... so I am tackling you. This is the black and white version of what you *need* to hear. No fluff added.

Know this, you are in grave danger, and it is my job as a believer in Jesus Christ, to make you aware of what is false and also what is required of you to go to Heaven. I feel like no one is grabbing us by the hand and telling us this information. This is why I am.

I know that if we had the power to mold our beliefs to suit certain world views, it would make this life so much easier to live.

However, spiritualism is a complete waste of time if your goal is to seek peace in the afterlife. STOP going down this road. All that you are doing is befriending evil spirits that will certainly take you down a road of no return.

James 2:19 "You believe that there is one God. You

do well. Even the demons believe—and tremble!"

Be assured that if you decide to follow New Age Spiritualism or progressive Christianity, you will absolutely get to the next life. But the promise of that life is eternal fire, pain, anguish, and no rest— ever. It is also known as Hell. Time to become awake.

1 Timothy 4:1-2 "But the Spirit explicitly says that in later times some will fall away from the faith, paying attention to deceitful spirits and teachings of demons, speaking lies in hypocrisy, having their own conscience seared with a hot iron,"

Jesus Christ is the ONLY path to the glorious next life, the new world known as Heaven.

Even if you don't believe anything I've said, I challenge you to investigate the teachings of spiritualism and the teachings of Jesus for yourself, and, at the very least, I hope I've triggered some scepticism about the practice of New Age Spiritualism. You have no idea how truly evil the forces that you are dabbling with, are. Take the time to look into it... it's crucial.

I know this might be really difficult to hear, but it's also very difficult to write. As I am writing, I'm thinking of many of my spiritually enlightened friends who fully embrace the practice. I don't want them to hate me for warning them about the dangers of what they're doing, because in reality, it all appears to be quite innocent.

Nonetheless, I am more concerned with their ultimate fate than with this life. The Bible does precisely what it should; it convicts us, causing us to change our ways and stop sinning.

If you are tempted to put this book down, please don't. Instead, have a conversation with God. And yet, you don't need me to convince you of his importance, because once you reach out to God, he will do that. ***HE has been patiently and lovingly waiting for you.***

Chapter Ten

The Promise Of Unbelievable Times

Inside the Bible's pages lie the answers to all the problems that mankind has ever known. I hope Americans will read and study the Bible.
– Ronald Reagan

The world. *Sigh*. Every single day we are seeing a new level of evil in our society. How has your experience been lately? Is it affecting your local community? Are you witnessing increased theft, growing anger, intense hate, and less concern for people in general? Or perhaps you recognize evil in other ways, such as on social media or on the news.

It seems that we have a rapid acceleration of bullying, intimidation, unjustified criticism, and hate happening. What is going on with us?

Besides this, I'm also observing the division of people. This is the most horrifying part to me. The old adage 'divide and conquer' rings eerily true in these times.

To add to the division, we are seeing increased health mandates, less healthcare, starvation, and many people are lacking the basic necessities of life. How is it that we continue to fail to provide the necessities of life to people all over the world? There is no excuse for this when there is so much wealth on earth.

Evil seems to be everywhere these days, and unfortunately, the government is no exception.

At first glance, you probably wouldn't consider what's happening in the political realm to be considered evil, but the government hierarchy is certainly playing a large evil role as well with their increasing overreach. As a result, we have seen the scale of fairness between multinational corporations and small businesses become very unbalanced.

The infiltration begins when the government wholeheartedly lends support to wealthy companies in order for them to increase their net worth with no concern for the consumers or small family-run businesses. These multinational corporations use deceptive marketing and undercut locally made products, all while poisoning us with crappy food and products made with hazardous materials.

Local businesses that provide much-needed services and support to the communities to which they belong have all but been forgotten by governments.

In the meantime, governments also lend support to the big corporate banks while these banks continue to make hundreds of millions of dollars in profits every year. And yet, those same banks that accept help from the government increasingly charge more service fees to their customers whose struggles are so great they simply can't afford to pay anymore.

What has happened to caring about actual people? You can't help but notice that people are no longer a priority for governments and big businesses. These days, everyone seems to be expendable, and companies will just 'fire your butt' and replace you no matter what your contribution has been to their company.

It's no longer about the 'mom and pop' businesses. It is about feeding corporate greed.

So, what is really going on?

These multinational companies are a new program in my lifetime. Companies used to have compassion for their employees, and especially their families. Families of employees used to be extremely important to companies because if they had happy employees, they also had productive and committed employees. Now, it is all about money, power, and the share-holders bottom line.

Well, my friends, this is Bible prophecy. No one is fixing this world. It's time to awaken your sleeping soul and open your blind eyes. Everything that is happening today is foretold in the Bible— believe it or choose not to.

2 Peter 3:4 They will say, "Where is the promise of his coming? For ever since the fathers fell asleep, all things are continuing as they were from the beginning of creation."

I recently realized that, I am, in reality, a terrible verbal communicator. When I try to communicate, I often get tongue-tied and can't get my thoughts out effectively. I've always aspired to be a writer, but to be honest, I never expected it would be about God.

My creative ambitions revolved around the outdoors and travel. I am an avid hiker and mountain biker. I adore the mountains and feel that I am closest to God when I am amongst them. Rather than thinking about composing a Christian book, I used to spend most of my spare time learning how to construct hiking blogs to share these beautiful places with people.

But I am a Christian. A Christian who was praying for discernment and guidance. And, as God would have it while praying one day and feeling near to Him, I felt a strong sense that God wanted me to write *this* book. I honestly didn't have a clue where to start, but nothing like jumping right into it.

I am still trying to figure things out, but here I am doing my best to hear God, and understand what my role is as a Christ follower. I feel as if God knows me, and more importantly, he knows we are not created equal.

Maybe this book is something that God planned to

use me for to grab the attention of people who would not normally give Christianity a second thought—because I can totally relate to that.

When I first began writing this book a year and a half ago, in the early months of 2021, I believed that I was creating a simple little book to catch the attention of those closest to me, to better explain my knowledge and convictions about God, again, because I'm a lousy verbal communicator.

But I now know that this book is intended for everyone who is struggling to understand God and the Bible, not only my friends and family. We need all the help we can get.

Christianity seems like a difficult concept to grasp because there is far too much inconsistency in the available information outside of the Bible. I am genuinely trying to be as clear as possible to help *you* understand because it's very difficult to have discussions about your beliefs with others without someone taking offence or brushing off what you are saying. I am trying to bring people together with God because he is our future.

Regrettably, I also sense the global division rapidly gaining ground. The Disciples of Jesus wrote about this in the New Testament. How did people of that day foresee so much of what would occur in the future? To those individuals in earlier civilizations, this was a complete foreign way of behavior.

Yet the answers to our future lie within the Bible,

in the inspired words of God. It's interesting how the Bible describes this subject in relation to the end times.

Luke 12:52-53 **"For from now on in one house there will be five divided, three against two and two against three. They will be divided, father against son, and son against father, mother against daughter, and daughter against the mother, mother-in-law against her daughter-in-law, and daughter-in-law against mother-in-law."**

Matthew 10:21-22 **"And the brother shall deliver up the brother to death, and the father the child: and the children shall rise up against *their* parents, and cause them to be put to death."**

If I had to look back at how I grew up in the 70's and 80's, I'd have to say life was pretty darn good.

I had a dad who always worked hard, two siblings who I got along with for the most part, and a mom who was always home after school... usually with a fresh batch of cookies for us kids. I always felt that I was part of a home filled with love and that my home was secure. I was never without any necessity of life, even though we didn't have many fancy things.

Throughout my entire childhood, I never once had to question the stability of my family.

So where did this all go wrong? Again, not to place blame on anyone because that truly helps no one, but I believe my generation played a big part in the transition from teaching children about loving God to loving-self. Self-love was the new catch phrase of this generation, and it has become so much worse with every generation forward.

I desperately wish that I could go back and teach my kids how to truly know and love God. This is my biggest regret in life. I screwed up and made choices that I knew were wrong at the time, I could feel it in my heart. Even though I was not genuinely close to God at the time, I could hear him in my conscience telling me the correct choices to make, but I ignored him. Undeniably, it was my choice to ignore Him, and so, life hasn't always been that easy for me.

But now that I have complete faith in God, I pray on a daily basis that he do his will rather than mine. I no longer want to be the decision maker. I know that God is way better at it than I am, and I am good with that because I totally trust him.

For some of you who are younger, this world is all that you have ever known. For some of you that are older, you have seen many changes happen.

In my case, fast forward to today.

In my short fifty-five years, I think... wow, I can't believe how quickly things have shifted in the world. Not in a million years would I have dreamt that I would be a witness to the human nastiness that is plaguing our world today.

It's not only the anxiety and impatience we seem to have with strangers, but today we are also experiencing it within the family dynamic. We are seeing many families torn apart by divided parents and unhealthy relationships, and it all begins with intolerance of each other, which is pretty surprising since our politically correct world revolves around tolerance these days.

So, I looked at some statistics.

Recent data on divorce describes the divorce rate as skyrocketing absolutely everywhere in the world. Surprisingly, however, the United States came in at number ten on the list at a 53% rate.

I know, shocking.

Most of us would tend to think that the U.S. should be number one, but they are not the highest by far. There are nine other countries that report between a 55% and 71% divorce rate, with Belgium being rated as the number one highest.

That's crazy! Just think about that. Almost three-quarters of all Belgian marriages end in divorce. What is happening to us?!

It is not my job to judge anyone or point fingers at them. There are many different reasons for divorce, and some of them are most certainly justified. I know people who have experienced horrific abuse in marriages, and they have no choice but to leave the abuser. I totally agree and understand this. The pain and anguish some people experience is very real, and it is a horrifying situation for the children as well.

However, according to multiple studies, the most reported causes of divorce were lack of commitment, conflict, and infidelity. I also believe that sometimes the decision to split-up is partially due to the promise of greener grass and an easier life. Regardless, an easier life is usually not the case after divorce. We are divorcing because we are not very happy.

But have we honestly done everything we can to change that unhappiness? Those promises (vows) that we make in our marriage ceremony are actually for those times when we *don't* feel love for one another. Those vows should be a reminder of the promises that we made on that special day when we committed to each other for life; but we have forgotten about the vows we made that day.

Sadly, the result of this increased divorce rate has undoubtedly affected the children of divorce, and then, those children's future families are most often impacted as well. It unmistakably spills into the next generation by quietly condoning future divorce by example. Instead of taking the more difficult road of staying committed and teaching your kids how to work through the 'good times and bad', we take the easier road of separating ourselves from the hard times.

As a result, the family unit has been redefined to suit the world and not the world redefined to suit the traditional family dynamic. Divorce is simply too simple, and traditional family values are facing increased hostility to make way for the new world ways.

Our young people are being trained to love themselves first— which never works well in a marriage.

So, if marriages are not working out, that's alright. Our attitude today is to just divorce and find someone else that will make us happier. Easy, right?

I encourage you; your marriages <u>are</u> worth it. Your family <u>is</u> worth it. Don't always take the easy road. Humble yourself, pray and ask God to bless your marriage instead of giving up.

I have been married for a *very* long time, and honestly, the majority of that time has not been super easy. As much as my husband and I seem to be alike because we do, in fact, have many of the same interests, we are both very different. And that's OK. The problem is that the difference is usually not totally realized until your kids are gone, and you suddenly have more time for yourself again.

This is the time when you rediscover who you are, especially if you were married at a young age like I was. This is also the time in life when a huge second wave of divorce happens— when the kids leave.

Personally, we are still sorting ourselves out after 36 years together, but we <u>are</u> sorting it out. Our commitment to each other includes a deep love and trust for each other, along with a mutual respect for the differences we have. That is what a marriage really is about. We depend on each other in ways that go far beyond mere friendships.

Why is it that we think our marriages are supposed to be filled with head over heels love all the time? This fantasy is so far from the truth. Even the best marriages are tested at some point in the relationship because we often become frustrated with the other person and start to lose patience.

This is usually the 'spark' for the fire that cannot be extinguished if both people don't fight it.

Real love is unconditional (agape) love. Agape love overlooks each other's shortcomings and faults, but this is a difficult thing to do because humans are naturally very selfish. Everything we do is a roundabout way to essentially get what *we* want and putting the other person first is not a priority most of the time. But this is how we should behave. This is how God wants us to behave... especially with our spouse.

Another issue that I find extremely concerning is that many of the younger generations are also choosing not to have children. This is a HUGE concern, that surprisingly, deeply worries our friend 'Elon' as well.

Here's what the data points to.

It seems that a portion of this phenomenon stems from young people feeling that it is increasingly difficult to find the 'perfect' partner.

The data also suggests that young people are much more concerned with their education, then having a great career, and maybe eventually starting a family when they are settled in life.

Unfortunately, for some, that perfect time doesn't always come, and then, suddenly, it's too late to have kids. Or possibly they have waited too long to find the perfect mate, who also might never come along.

Another factor driving this childless future is the cost of having kids. Kids are expensive, and increased uncertainty in the job market has caused people to feel unsure about providing financial stability for a family. This is a very real concern. I understand how they feel.

Also, according to the data, yet another disturbing trend is happening. Some young people feel that the world is such a horrible place with all of its 'climate crisis' that they do not want to bring children into this crisis world.

What kind of horrible fear have we instilled in our children to convince them that they should not have children and that it is in the best interest of the world to not have any more new inhabitants.

These young people have no idea of the joy children can bring to them, and also, what they will miss as old people, being all alone. You can never have these moments back.

God instructed us to have children, lots of them, and has never told us to stop because of climate change or not having the perfect house. Please seriously consider having a family.

There also seems to be plenty of underlying pressure from society itself, encouraging young people to seriously consider whether or not to bring kids into this world and add to the demand on the world's resources. Depending on where you live, this influence will vary, but it still concerns me that this miraculous gift of life is taken so lightly. Children are seen as a blessing in the eyes of God, and we absolutely require young people to continue having kids for many reasons.

As Elon puts it, "Too many good, smart people think that there are too many people in the world and the population is growing out of control. But it's completely the opposite." He urged people to look at the data and said, "If people don't have more children, civilization is going to crumble." He also said, "Mark his words."

However, the most selfish reason in the studies for young adults to make the choice not to have children... is just that. Young people are choosing not to have children because they themselves are selfish. There is no hiding the fact that kids are a lot of work. So, if you happen to be selfish, any children you have could potentially disrupt the prospective parents' lives and careers. Less *me* time, I suppose.

I think what the younger generation fails to realize at a young age, is that when you become older, your kids and grandkids become your entire world. None of the things we thought were important as young people are a concern when you are older. Those used to be important things are no longer a priority, and your family becomes everything.

God has given us enough resources to survive. Our problem is that we are really lousy at sharing them.

Again, I am not judging anyone for their choices. I am merely pointing out what the available data reflects on this subject and the reasons behind it. Please deeply consider your choices. Kids really are an amazing gift.

I remember thinking not all that long ago about the foretold future prophecies that the Bible talks about, and I thought to myself, how is all of that stuff that the Bible says is going to happen, actually going to happen? In my world view at the time, I could not imagine the world of today. None of us could. All we knew was the world we grew up in. Heck... I couldn't even imagine this world five years ago.

Yet here we are, drawing ever closer to the foretold prophecies in the Bible, however, these fulfillments of prophecies have been going on unannounced for quite some time. They are now accelerating more quickly.

For example, the Bible speaks about the last days and perilous times to come. But before any of that stuff could happen, some other events needed to come to fruition first, and one of those particular events, was the re-gathering of the Jewish people.

The Jewish people had been scattered from their homeland, Israel, since the time before Jesus' birth. Now I know... this does not seem like a big deal, but the fact that these Jewish people have remained true to their lineage for over two thousand years, despite not having a homeland for thousands of years, is a miracle in and of itself.

Think of us being kicked out of our country. We likely wouldn't all go to the same place. Chances are we would have been dispersed throughout the world and ended up adapting to the new countries we were now in— especially after a hundred years.

This is similar to new immigrants coming to our country. Chances are good that the succeeding generations would hardly know anything about the country their relatives were kicked out of because they would no longer be connected to it.

Yet, the Israelites stayed true to their lineage. They not only continued with their traditions but also remembered their God.

Recognize that they no longer had a community like they used to because they had been scattered throughout the world for over two thousand years.

So why is this so important?

Well, in May of 1948, Israel, once again became a nation after twenty-five hundred years of not being one.

Then, in 1967, during the Six Day War, the Israelites overcame great military odds to re-capture the Temple Mount in Jerusalem. The Temple Mount is a very important religious area that the Jewish people lost in 586 B.C. Ezekiel's prophecy (from the Bible) of this recapturing event was foretold around twenty-five hundred years ago.

Well, that's cool... but what is the connection?

Incredibly, these events were foretold prophecies

in the Old Testament of the Bible, and actually came true in 1948 and 1967. In our lifetime, essentially. This was not only a miracle of God that came true as it was foretold, but it also again proves the absolute truth of the written word of God in the Bible.

Zechariah 8:7-8 This is what the Lord Almighty says: "I will save my people from the countries of the east and the west. I will bring them back to live in Jerusalem; they will be my people, and I will be faithful and righteous to them as their God."

The Bible also foretells that in the future we will take the 'Mark of the Beast.' No one knows exactly what this will be, and really, who can comprehend how this is going to happen? This seems impossible. Why on earth would anyone volunteer for something such as this? And how could anyone be forced to accept this mark?

Until recently, we lived in a very free society. The taking of the 'mark' did not seem possible anytime soon. But here we are today, rapidly losing our freedoms and I can hardly believe what has happened in the past year… the past two years. This scripture is becoming a reality before our very eyes, a very vivid real-life reality.

However, we do not know the exact time, so it could be a very long way away... or a very short time away. Only God knows this one.

Revelation 13:16-17 "It also forced all people, great

and small, rich and poor, free and slave, to receive a mark on their right hands or on their foreheads, so that they could not buy or sell unless they had the mark, which is the name of the beast or the number of its name."

Matthew 24:42 "Therefore, stay awake, for you do not know on what day your Lord is coming."

As I learn more and more of what has been foretold in the Bible about the times to come, the prophecies and scripture make so much sense now. The Bible is pretty straight-up about what is going to happen, and even though we won't want to face these up-and-coming things, it cannot be any other way before the return of Christ. They have to happen.

Evil definitely oversees this world, and God has told us that in the 'end times' evil will take full control. It's happening.

As much as we'd like to think *we* have control, we don't. Evil will be here until Jesus returns.

More importantly, remember that, 'The Day of the Lord' comes as a thief in the night. Be prepared.

Luke 12:39-40 "But understand this: If the homeowner had known at what hour the thief was coming, he would not have let his house be broken into. You also must be ready, because the Son of Man will come at an hour you do not expect."

I never imagined in my lifetime that I would see

these biblical events happen— and maybe I still won't see them all. But if you understand the current times and the Bible, Christ is promised to soon return. That could mean tomorrow, or that could mean one hundred and fifty years from now. All we really know is that there <u>will</u> be a judgement day when every single person will have to answer to God.

So why is this important today?

Well, in the Bible, the prophecies describe how God foretold of these 'end times' that we are experiencing right now, and incredibly, all these unbelievable things that are going on can be referenced in the Bible.

But before you become extremely anxious about the coming wrath, you need to realize that the return of Jesus is for our salvation. Jesus is rescuing us *from* evil. Which is amazing if you choose to believe in God. Not so great... if you don't.

I am convinced we are living in the 'last days' as described by Jesus and the Bible. This is why I am telling you this. There are far too many people in this world who EXPECT to go to heaven... but instead will end up in hell.

I know, this is hard to hear, and you think I'm crazy. I don't blame you. I think it sounds nuts too. But I challenge you to look up everything that I have said for yourself. Find your own answers to these questions. It is imperative that you do. Closely examine what is happening all over the world at this moment. Could this scripture possibly relate to our world today?

2 Timothy 3:1-7 "But understand this, that in the last days there will come times of difficulty. For people will be lovers of self, lovers of money, proud, arrogant, abusive, disobedient to their parents, ungrateful, unholy, heartless, unappeasable, slanderous, without self-control, brutal, not loving good, treacherous, reckless, swollen with conceit, lovers of pleasure rather than lovers of God, having the appearance of godliness but denying its power. Avoid such people. For among them are those who creep into households and capture weak women, burdened with sins and led astray by various passions, always learning and never able to arrive at a knowledge of the truth."

Just know, that the Time of Tribulation spoken about in the Book of Revelation (the last chapter of the Bible) is coming. Jesus tells us over and over to 'fear not'. You know why? Because evil can't touch Him. Trust Him because God trumps all evil.

I am not a conspiracy theorist. The world loves to label people who tell the truth because what they say is outside of the modern world view. Use your own critical thinking and don't accept what you are being told without first educating yourself with the facts.

Ask yourself, "What actually makes sense?" Don't simply tow the trendy line. Think for yourself before it's too late to do this.

This modern worldview is not of God. So, if it's

not of God, it's of Satan. It makes total sense for disbelievers to say hateful things about people who disagree with them.

I love the fact that these people also try to put anyone outside of their worldview in a box. These are the same people who say we shouldn't label people.

But here is some news for them… you *cannot* put God in a BOX.

This spiritual warfare is not a war over physical things in this world. This is a war for control of your mind. Satan wants to control what we think and then imprison us with those beliefs.

The bottom line for me is that even if all this effort only plants a seed in one person to seek the truth about Jesus Christ, all the long hours of studying and writing will be worth it.

At the absolute least, I hope that this book causes you to contemplate the recent events around the world and that you've started to realize that God *is* absolutely real, and that Jesus is ***undoubtedly your saviour.***

Chapter Eleven
The Promise
Of God

"Every word of God proves true; he is a
shield to those who take refuge in him"
Proverbs 30:5

What is the promise of God? God has many promises, but the one in particular that we should pay close attention to is the promise of 'fierce wrath upon men' because not only has God promised many things, but he has *always* delivered on his promises as well.

Luke 21:25-26 **"And there will be signs in sun and moon and stars, and on the earth distress of nations in perplexity because of the roaring of the sea and the waves, people fainting with fear and with foreboding of what is coming on the world. For the powers of the heavens will be shaken."**

In this chapter, I will explain what the Bible has to say about the four major things that are foretold to happen in the future:

1) There will be a seven year Time of Tribulation
2) The Antichrist will be revealed
3) The Rapture of the Church
4) The return of Jesus

Revelation 20:12-15 "And I saw the dead, small and great, stand before God; and the books were opened, which is the book of life; and the dead were judged out of those things which were written in the books, according to their works. And the sea gave up the dead which were in it; and death and hell delivered up the dead which were in them; and they were judged every man according to their works. And death and hell were cast into the lake of fire. This is the second death. And whosoever was not found written in the book of life was cast into the lake of fire."

What's next? As I learn more about what is happening in the world today, God's plan becomes more and more clear. The frightening part is that the time of Great Tribulation seems to be coming quickly. So, my thoughts turn to: Are we prepared for this time? What can we do?

I truly hope I'm wrong, but I feel like we are running out of time. Jesus told us that we wouldn't know the exact time, but we would be aware of the signs of the times.

The prophetic word in the Bible also warns us of things not yet seen. That is, while most of us will not understand everything that is going on, we will be aware of it soon. Understand that this fight is spiritual warfare, and it is very real.

The Bible says to be cognizant of the coming Time of Tribulation. This is a seven-year period where human depravity will have reached its peak, and at a certain point in this time, God will pour out His wrath upon us.

Daniel 12:1 "At that time Michael shall stand up, the great prince who stands watch over the sons of your people; And there shall be a time of trouble, such as never was since there was a nation, even to that time. And at that time your people shall be delivered, every one who is found written in the book."

1) The Time of Tribulation: The Tribulation is going to mark the beginning of a seven-year period when God will finish the discipline of his people of Israel, and also finalize his judgement of the unbelieving world. This time will occur just prior to the return of Christ.

Matthew 24:21 "For then there will be a great tribulation, such as has not occurred since the beginning of the world until now, nor ever shall be."

During the first three and a half years of the Tribulation, do not be fooled. This time is foretold to have peace and prospering within it as the world gets some relief. However, this time of peace is short and does not last, and things will suddenly change for the worse... much worse.

It is said in the Bible that after that time of the first three and a half years, the time of the 'Great' Tribulation will be upon us, and God's full wrath will be 'poured out' upon the people. The remaining three and a half years are described as being almost unbearable for the world. If we think it's bad now, just wait until this time.

Matthew 24:12 "And because lawlessness will be increased, the love of many will grow cold."

We are also promised a One World Government, a One World Currency, a One World Religion and a falling away of believers. The groundwork for these things is already being laid today. Let's break these times down:

A One World Government: As we speak, we are losing the military might of the world's most powerful country, the USA. It is obvious that this nation is also becoming a weaker nation in general. For the first time in a very long time, we can see that the USA might not be the 'superpower' for much longer.

Inflation is now also at levels rarely seen, and we are

told of even more serious shortages of fuel, food, and other products coming in the near future. Some of these shortages we have already been experiencing, and they are beginning to affect our lives in some way or another.

Besides shortages of food and goods, the pandemic has also pushed all the nation's leaders to act as tyrants, forcing mandates on people's rights and freedoms.

As a result of these events, the military and economic meltdown might very well 'trigger' an action that will then gather all nations to band together in order to initiate the Great Reset of the world. This is an event that the world's elites are seeking. In other words, a One World Government is no longer an impossible reality. It is actually in our near future.

Matthew 24:6 "And you will hear of wars and rumours of wars. See that you are not alarmed, for this must take place, but the end is not yet."

A One World Currency: With the necessary decline of 'real' physical money and the progression to digital currency happening, we can certainly see how a One World Currency is on the horizon. China has already moved to a digital system, and because the entire world trades with China, all of the other nations will soon follow suit.

A digital currency system would also allow governments to manage the ever-increasing debt they have accumulated by wiping away individual country currencies and replacing it with a world wide universal digital currency.

Add to this, the highly transmissible pandemic and the chance of passing illness through the exchange of tangible money. We can now see a near certain future without real money.

Cash will be removed for our 'safety' but this will also provide an opportunity for governments to monitor our spending habits. We will never again be able to do anything anonymously after this, they will hold all the cards.

With great technological advances in digital tracking and artificial intelligence, we can legitimately see a future 'Mark' being imposed on us for buying or selling. This digital system will also give the government more control. This is not speculation.

These systems are already in place and being used. For example, China already has a social credit style system where individuals are allotted points for good behaviour and deducted points for going against what the government deems to be OK. The fewer points you have, the less freedoms you have.

China's citizens also cannot escape being monitored by the more than 200 million CCTV cameras in their country. Some reports say that the number may be closer to 800 million— and the US is catching up. Through artificial intelligence, Big Brother will always be watching in the future.

A One World Religion and falling away of

believers: Religion has been falling away in the developed world for quite a long time now, and the age of supposed tolerance is upon us. Whether it is evil or good, we are told to just shut-up and celebrate what society has deemed as right... not God.

All the other religions in the world will also become less prevalent due to the forthcoming One World Religion that will likely emphasize inclusivity, socialism, and the climate. Everyone seems to want to be inclusive in today's world, no matter how much it goes against what the Bible teaches. The world has a total disregard for God.

These groups will also seek the true Christian churches' destruction and Christians who refuse to worship the image of the Beast will be martyred. It will be seen as a 'good thing' for humanity. In other words, the killing of Christians will be celebrated.

Matthew 24:7-14 "For nation will rise against nation, and kingdom against kingdom, and there will be famines and earthquakes in various places. All these are but the beginnings of birth pains. Then shall they deliver you up to tribulation and put you to death, and you will be hated by all nations for my name's sake. And then many will fall away and betray one another. And many false prophets will arise and lead many astray. And because lawlessness will be increased, the love of many will grow cold. But the one who endures to the end will be saved. And this gospel of the

kingdom will be proclaimed throughout the whole world as a testimony to all nations, and then the end will come."

Does this scripture sound familiar? People are already being labelled as domestic terrorists for questioning authorities— and we are just getting started. The foundation is being laid for all of this right now. Open your eyes.

1 Thessalonians 5:6 "So let us not sleep, as do others, but let us keep awake and be sober."

2) The Antichrist: What role does the Antichrist play in this end time? Throughout history, there have been numerous antichrists, but the one at the time of tribulation refers to the last antichrist. By far the most powerful.

When we hear the phrase 'antichrist,' we immediately think of someone dressed up as the antichrist... an evil figure. Hitler has been referred to as the antichrist by some.

However, in actuality, the last antichrist will most likely be someone that people admire. He may appear almost too wonderful to be true and be praised; being promoted to a position of power and, providing us with temporary tranquility.

2 Thessalonians 2:9-10 "The coming of the lawless one is by the activity of Satan with all power and false signs and wonders, and with all wicked

deception for those who are perishing, because they refused to love the truth and so be saved."

Who will this person of the New World Order be? The truth is, we don't know. But he will be someone who will have extraordinary powers, and it will seem like he can also mimic the power of Jesus and set himself up to be 'like' God.

OK, come on, really?

Yes, this is what Jesus taught— as well as the Bible.

The antichrist will come to test the saints and the church, to see who truly is faithful to Christ. But in order to deceive us, the Antichrist will have the power to do similar things as Jesus did when he was alive on earth two-thousand years ago.

This isn't an assumption. This is well documented in the Bible and is not primarily written only in the Old Testament text either, it is in both the New and Old Testaments.

Pay close attention when you see a new leader of the world emerging. He will be the 'great deceiver' who is going to prosper in the power of Satan and demand to be worshipped. It is also said that he will speak 'marvelous' things to us that will deceive many, many people. To these people, the Antichrist will resemble the return of Jesus. Resist worshipping this person with everything you have. When it is the real Jesus, all eyes will see him.

Remember, God does not promise that only <u>some</u> of the Bible prophecies will come true. He promises that everything will happen as he has said it will.

Matthew 24:23-27 "Then if anyone says to you, 'Look, here is the Christ!' or 'There he is!' do not believe it. For false christs and false prophets will arise and perform great signs and wonders, so as to lead astray, if possible, even the elect. See, I have told you beforehand. So, if they say to you, 'Look, he is in the wilderness,' do not go out. If they say, 'Look, he is in the inner rooms,' do not believe it. For as the lightning comes from the east and shines as far as the west, so will be the coming of the Son of Man."

#3) The Rapture of Christ's Church: If you've never heard of the 'Rapture' and don't understand what it means, it means that the people who have trusted and believed (true Christian Saints) in the person of Jesus Christ are suddenly taken away to be with Jesus in order to save them from the remaining punishment to come.

I know what you're thinking again, "That's pretty far-fetched. How will this happen?"

The truth is, no one really knows for sure because nothing like this has ever happened before. But God promises the people of His church to be 'taken up' in an instant, so they are not present during the most difficult times when the 'Wrath of God' comes.

I'm certain we will witness a well-orchestrated coming 'cosmic delusion' at this time to explain the sudden disappearance of a lot of people on Earth, but how are the remaining people on earth going to comprehend the fact that so many people have suddenly disappeared?

Well, if you are familiar with the ways of evil, look around at what is going on with deception in the world. You will clearly see that the followers of Satan are setting the world up for an explanation. I know this sounds crazy, but deception and the conditioning of humans is a very real thing, and now there is so much deception and lying in this world, we rarely know what the truth is anymore. I honestly wouldn't put it past the 'powers that be' to use something such as a 'UFO' to explain the Rapture of the Church.

Just take notice... even right now, of what is being pushed in the media with regard to alien life forms. Our universe is so massive! People have no idea of what is truly out there. But already, there are millions of people who believe, one hundred percent, that there is alien life out there, even without any real evidence.

These people reason to themselves that we can't possibly be the only ones in our universe. And if you look at it through their eyes, because of what the media portrays, it's not too hard to imagine that an alien life form could exist. In fact, over fifty percent of the world's population already believes in extraterrestrial life.

Well, isn't that just convenient.

And so, because people already believe in this stuff, society won't require much convincing for a rapture to be explained away with UFO's and aliens.

Pay attention in the future to all the constantly emerging new video evidence that you will be seeing. It will be difficult to ignore.

So, if UFOs are fake, how are we seeing videos of them?

Good question.

I think what we fail to realize is that the technology for this type of deception has been readily available for quite some time. Remember who's leading this parade... Satan is described in the Bible as the ultimate deceiver.

Also, think about what God says about his amazing creation. God states very clearly that he is the creator of the universe. So, if God is the creator of everything, including the sun, moon, and stars, and if God did not say anything about aliens in his creation, then why are we convinced that there is such a thing as alien life? In fact, God teaches us about this very deception from Satan in the end times.

4) The return of Jesus: At the time of the Great Tribulation comes the Day of the Lord. Here is the good news: Jesus is coming back soon. Not only to make things right in this world, but also to see his creation flourish as it should have from the start. I definitely want to be a part of that. We all have an opportunity to be a part of it. It's a choice we make.

Look around at what is happening. The violence on earth is ever increasing, just as Jesus said it was going to happen, and the world is purging the love of God out of it. Like un-tolerant tolerance in the name of whatever society has deemed correct to rid the world of God.

Matthew 24: 29-30 "Immediately after the tribulation of those days . . . the Son of Man will appear in the sky, and then all the tribes of the earth will mourn, and they will see the Son of Man coming on the clouds of the sky with power and great glory."

The Bible also assures us that Jesus' return is imminent; the only question is when. We can't escape it, and we can't wish away. It will simply take place. Our Father, God, is the only one who knows the precise moment. Take notice and <u>read</u> the Bible.

Matthew 24:36 "But concerning that day and hour no one knows, not even the angels of heaven, nor the Son, but the Father only"

Matthew 24:43 "But know this, that if the master of the house had known in what part of the night the thief was coming, he would have stayed awake and would not have let his house be broken into."

Luke 12:40 "You also must be ready, for the Son of Man is coming at an hour you do not expect."

We will *all* be at 'Judgement Day' whether you choose to believe this or not. It doesn't matter if we are dead or alive at that time, our everlasting soul will be judged on that day. God has not lied about any other promise so far, so I wouldn't be so certain that you'll be spared his wrath.

How could any one of us overcome the all powerful Creator of us. It's not going to happen. This world is a diabolical mess. God knows what he's doing. Trust His words.

Please consider what I have said. Your eternity depends on it. God has warned us, the Bible has warned us, and Jesus has warned us. ***This day is fast approaching.***

Chapter Twelve
How To Expect Heaven...

"Now faith is the assurance of things hoped for, the conviction of things not seen."
Hebrews 11:1

So, why am I doing this, knowing I will have my share of haters that will voice their opinions?

Simply because, this is the job of being a Christ follower. God's wish is to not lose one single soul, and as a Christian, I am required to tell people the truth. This is more important than making friends, being popular, or achieving success... and let me tell you, it has taken me way too long to realize this.

Believe me, this is not the way to win a popularity contest. I have been a Christ follower for over twenty years, and not so surprisingly, most of my friends don't know this fact about me. I rarely talk about my beliefs with anyone for fear of offending someone or being hated.

Stigma is most definitely associated with Christianity, and it is challenging to be separated from that stigma once people realize that you are actually someone who believes in God. Once found out, people act differently and treat you differently. I can't figure it out because I am the same person that I was last week when you didn't know I was a Christian. Yet, you act differently now.

I also feared that certain individuals would decide not to be a 'friend' any longer because I might be considered way out there with my convictions and old-fashioned with my beliefs. I like to call them, traditional beliefs— similar to the beliefs our grandparents had.

Truthfully, I can only be as tolerant as God allows me to be and not accept what I deem is right. Correctness must come from the rule maker, who is God, and unfortunately, that doesn't fly in today's *everything is OK* culture.

But you know what, it's finally OK with me. I am over it. I work for God now. I hope you can see that God needs to be the most important thing in *all* of our lives.

Proverbs 3:5-6 "Trust in the Lord with all your heart and lean not on your own understanding. In all your ways acknowledge him and he will make straight your paths."

Matthew 10:38-39 "And anyone who does not take up his cross and follow Me is not worthy of Me. Whoever finds his life will lose it, and whoever loses his life for My sake will find it."

Think of it like this: If I knew you had a damaged brake line on your car, and I knew that meant you didn't have brakes, and I was sure you were going to drive that car down that steep hill with the cliff at the bottom. And I knew without a doubt, that if I didn't warn you, you'd be killed. Then I'd be the one credited for your death.

The same is true of authentic Christianity. This is how I would feel if I kept all of Jesus' information to myself. How could I not warn anyone about what I know is going to happen if I sincerely loved and cared for people as a true Christian? Jesus told us to put our faith solely in him, and he also told us to warn others if they were unaware of how to be saved.

Even though I feel I have always sensed God's presence, I haven't always behaved like a person who believes in God should. I'm a long way away from being perfect. I literally cannot stand the person I used to be, and, I'm still working on the person I am now.

I wasn't what you'd call a 'very good' believer at the time. In my life, things were quite intense, and I had a lot of anxiety that ultimately piqued one day. So, out of sheer desperation, I pleaded with God to help me. To my surprise and wonder… He did. It was at that point I recognized God was real, and I received him into my life. There are no other words to explain what has occurred in my life. That was over two decades ago.

I often thought about God over those twenty-two years, but I was too scared to really commit to him. For the longest time, I didn't want to say to God, 'use me' because I was terrified of what that meant, and how it would change my life— because I just knew it would.

Plus, I was still doing things that would not have pleased Him. But I believe that everything happens for His reason, and the events of the past make perfect sense to me now, as does me writing this book.

God often uses many of his people as pastors or preachers. Others may go on to act as missionaries in other countries or serve on church councils that help the poor. That wasn't really my deal, and God knows this. But I was certain that God wanted me to serve in some capacity… I just couldn't imagine how. Now I know.

Ya, a shocker for me too.

I sincerely hope and pray that Jesus saves everyone, however, I am aware that some of you will be doubtful of what I have written. These words will almost certainly make these people laugh out loud.

I get it, this is a lot to absorb. But I would rather offend you to Heaven, than comfort you to Hell.

The Bible is an enormous book, but it is not an out-of-date book filled with just good suggestions; it is the final authority on life, and you can't deny that it entirely makes sense because there are no inconsistencies within it— unlike evolution.

I'm telling you the truth with grace and honesty. Please seriously consider what I have said. What could have possibly motivated me to put myself out there and tell you these things? I didn't spend over a year and a half of my life studying and writing because I feel like being unpopular— or hated. In this world, we all want to be loved and popular.

However, the world is rarely fair, and it tells endless lies. The world isn't good… **GOD IS.**

I am writing this book and trying to convince you to not let your soul be stolen by Satan for eternity. It is not cool to give up your soul for such a short-term gain in this world. Seriously sift my testimony and test my integrity. I guarantee that you will come to the same conclusion, which is critical for discovering the truth.

Consider that each day before I begin writing, I pray and ask God that whatever words come to my mind come from him… not from me. I am <u>not</u> at the mercy of doubters…I am at the mercy of God.

I did not write one word of this book on my own. I honestly don't have the patience. Because like you, I too *am* selfish. I would rather be hiking, or riding my mountain bike, or skiing, gardening, boating, painting a wall.... *anything* really, other than sitting down and writing for months on end.

But here I am, writing a book because the Holy Spirit of God moved me to do so. I truly cannot explain it…**other than God.**

So, what does the future hold for me? I honestly have no idea, but I'm not worried because I believe God and his words.

Whatever the next stage of this emerging crazy evil world becomes, I will not deny God, Jesus, or the Holy Spirit anymore, because without them, I don't have a future... and you don't either.

When we put our faith in Jesus, the Holy Spirit comes to us as a helper. Sincerely pray that the Holy Spirit stays with you every single day— you are going to need him. God loves you and is trying to influence you to choose him. In the same way Satan is also tying to influence your choice.

Remember, all of this is a choice. God does NOT send us to Hell. We go there by our own choice. Out of pure love for us, God gave us the freedom to make our own choices. Stop assuming that all of this is impossible. It is not, and your arrogance will ultimately kill you.

Stop rationalizing everything in today's worldview, God doesn't have the same tools as us. His are much more amazing than ours.

The bottom line is this… am I saying that *unless* you accept Jesus Christ as your Lord and Saviour, you will go to Hell? And am I saying that there is no *other* way to enter Heaven except through Jesus? Am I also saying you *cannot* enter Heaven through any other religion? YES, I am.

Actually... I lied. I am _not_ saying anything. **GOD *is* saying this in the Bible**.

Ask God the question and pray. Pray that God opens your heart and reveals Jesus to you. I can one hundred percent guarantee that He _will_ answer you.

One thing is absolutely certain, ten out of ten of us are going to die. No one escapes death. The good news is that when you truly know God and Jesus, death is no longer terrifying.

The Bible says the wages of sin is death. Every single day, one hundred and fifty-thousand people die. Which day will you die? Are you ready?

However, this is the BEST part of all, according to the Bible, evil has absolutely no authority over Jesus Christ and God. God is the master of all, so why would you settle for anything less?

May God bless you. I'll be praying for you...

"You will seek me and find me, when you seek me with all your heart."
Jeremiah 29:13

Acknowledgement

Thank you to my Lord and Saviour, Jesus Christ, who is with me always. Also, thanks to my loving husband, who was *mostly* patient during the year and a half it took to write this book. Let's go hiking.